EUROPEAN SOCIOLOGY

HOW THE LABOURER LIVES

A STUDY OF THE RURAL LABOUR PROBLEM

B. SEEBOHM ROWNTREE

AND

MAY KENDALL

ARNO PRESS

A New York Times Company

New York — 1975

Reprint Edition 1975 by Arno Press Inc.

Copyright © 1913, Thomas Nelson and Sons

Reprinted by permission of the
  Joseph Rowntree Charitable Trust

Reprinted from a copy in
  The University of Illinois Library

EUROPEAN SOCIOLOGY
ISBN for complete set: 0-405-06493-4
See last pages of this volume for titles.

Manufactured in the United States of America

———◆———

Library of Congress Cataloging in Publication Data

Rowntree, Benjamin Seebohm, 1871-1954.
    How the labourer lives.

    (European sociology)
    Reprint of the 1913 ed. published by T. Nelson,
London.
    Includes index.
    1. Cost and standard of living--Great Britain.
2. Agricultural laborers--Great Britain. I. Kendall,
May, joint. author. II. Title. III. Series.
HD7023.R7 1975   339.4'2   74-25780
ISBN 0-405-06533-7

HOW THE LABOURER LIVES

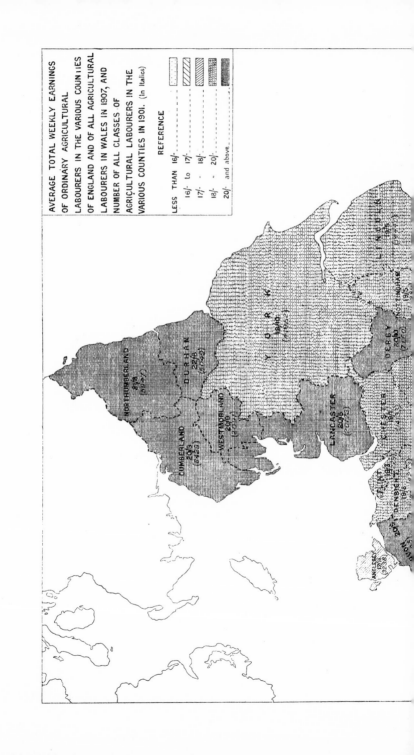

AVERAGE TOTAL WEEKLY EARNINGS OF ORDINARY AGRICULTURAL LABOURERS IN THE VARIOUS COUNTIES OF ENGLAND AND OF ALL AGRICULTURAL LABOURERS IN WALES IN 1907, AND NUMBER OF ALL CLASSES OF AGRICULTURAL LABOURERS IN THE VARIOUS COUNTIES IN 1901. (In Italics)

REFERENCE

LESS THAN 16/-
16/- to 17/-
17/- " 18/-
18/- " 20/-
20/- and above

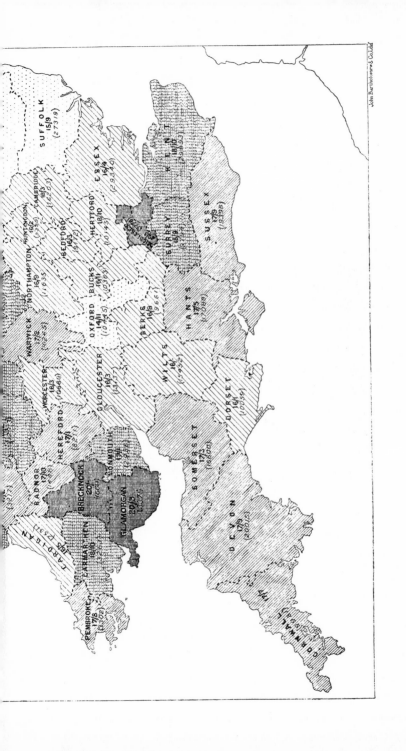

CARDIGAN
17/5
(25.11)

CARMARTHEN
18/10
(27.71)

PEMBROKE
17/8
(23.02)

BRECKNOCK
20/-
(6.54)

GLAMORGAN
20/0
(35.75)

RADNOR
17/10
(2.88)

HEREFORD
17/1
(8.711)

WORCESTER
16/3
(10.689)

MONMOUTH
19/
(16.0)

SOMERSET
17/2
(06.00)

DEVON
17/9
(202.13)

CORNWALL
19/1
(92.60)

DORSET
17/5
(10.59)

WILTS
16/-
(19.52)

GLOUCESTER
16/3
(13.33)

OXFORD
14/11
(10.415)

BERKS
16/8
(9.66)

HANTS
17/5
(10.89)

WARWICK
17/2
(10.24.5)

NORTHAMPTON
16/9
(11.635)

BUCKS
16/11
(9.363)

BEDFORD
16/3
(9.47)

HERTFORD
18/10
(10.145)

HUNTINGDON
16/2
(5.336)

CAMBRIDGE
16/3
(16.20.1)

SUFFOLK
15/9
(27.31.9)

ESSEX
14/4
(17.98.0)

SURREY
18/9
(12.8.93)

KENT
18/10
(28.8.93)

SUSSEX
17/9
(12.398)

John Bartholomew & Co. Ltd.

HOW THE LABOURER LIVES

A STUDY OF THE RURAL LABOUR PROBLEM

BY

B. SEEBOHM ROWNTREE

AUTHOR OF "POVERTY: A STUDY OF TOWN LIFE"
"LAND AND LABOUR: LESSONS FROM BELGIUM"
ETC.

AND

MAY KENDALL

THOMAS NELSON AND SONS

LONDON, EDINBURGH, DUBLIN, MANCHESTER, LEEDS
PARIS, LEIPZIG, MELBOURNE, AND NEW YORK

PREFACE.

The problems and the prospects of the worker on the land have of late aroused so much discussion that the British public is beginning to realize that the welfare of the village labourer is essential to the welfare of the nation as a whole.

There have been a number of recent contributions to the literature on this subject, but it seemed that there was room for a strictly unbiassed study of the actual economic position of the ordinary agricultural labourer with his present wage and outlook.

We have therefore applied to this class the method of measuring the standard of comfort, and especially the adequacy of the food consumed, already used in previous studies.

The first chapter gives a general survey of the situation, the size of the agricultural population, the migration of the labourer to the towns, and emigration to non-European countries.

Chapter II. contains the most recent statistics

of agricultural wages, and the extent to which they constitute a " living wage " is discussed.

The bulk of the book, however, consists of a number of household budgets which we have obtained in different districts. The detailed descriptions of each family will, we hope, give the reader the sense of intimate personal contact with facts which statistics alone do not always convey.

In the concluding chapter we have sketched our general impression of the agricultural labourer's life and of his own outlook. It is written after some hundreds of visits to labourers' homes in many parts of the country, and in the hope that it may help the reader to appreciate the meaning of inadequate wages in terms of sober reality.

We are grateful to those who have given us so many intimate details of their daily life and glimpses of their mental attitude. We wish to thank Mr. J. D. Roney-Dougal for supplying the material for studies Nos. 8, 12, and 33 ; Mr. B. Lasker for his criticism ; and Mr. F. D. Stuart for his statistical help.

YORK, *April* 1913.   M. K.

                                        B. S. R.

CONTENTS.

HOW THE LABOURER LIVES.

CHAPTER I.

INTRODUCTORY.

How to stop the steady drift of the population to the towns ?

That problem has a large place in the thought, not only of the English people, but of all the Western European countries. In England, how- ever, it has become so acute that it can no longer be shelved while " more urgent " matters receive attention, for here the urbanization of the popu- lation has proceeded further than in any other European country.

The problem is one of great complexity, and in this book we only consider one of the many factors which contribute to it. We shall not touch on such important questions as the system of land tenure, rural education, small holdings, or the relative advantages to agriculturists of Free Trade and Protection. We merely attempt to give a picture, drawn from life, of the actual conditions under which one section of the agricultural population, the labourers, are living. Even this subject we shall not exhaust; such salient factors as the condition and shortage of cottages will only incidentally be touched upon.

We must, however, begin by giving a few general facts and figures, so that the reader may realize the importance, from the national standpoint, of clearly grasping the present problem of the agricultural labouring class.

The first fact of which we will remind the reader is that whereas sixty years ago the population of England and Wales was evenly divided between town and country dwellers, now four out of every five persons are living in the towns, and only one out of five in the country.

This townward drift of the population has been steadily proceeding ever since there were census figures to reveal it, as may readily be seen by a glance at the following table:—

	Population of England and Wales residing in *			
Year.	Urban Districts.		Rural Districts.	
	Number.	Per cent.	Number.	Per cent.
1851 .	8,990,809	50·2	8,936,800	49·8
1861 .	10,960,998	54·6	9,105,226	45·4
1871 .	14,041,404	61·8	8,670,862	38·2
1881 .	17,636,646	67·9	8,337,793	32·1
1891 .	20,895,504	72·0	8,107,021	28·0
1901 .	25,058,355	77·0	7,469,488	23·0
1911 .	28,162,936	78·1	7,907,556	21·9

For the first three decades the figures have been estimated by the census authorities, and even in the case of later figures administrative changes make the comparison of one decade with another somewhat unreliable. But when full allowance has been made for all inaccuracies, the fact of the steady townward drift of the population remains unchallenged.

* Cd. 6,258, p. xvi.

It will be noticed that while the percentage of the rural population decreased on the average by about 5½ per cent. in each decade up to 1901, the decline during the succeeding ten years was only 1·1 per cent. Indeed, after an uninterrupted fall in the absolute number of the inhabitants of rural districts for fifty years (from 9 millions in 1851 to 7½ millions in 1901), the census for 1911 shows an increase of 10 per cent. These figures, however, do not necessarily point to a corresponding check of the flow of labour from agriculture to industry. In order to ascertain whether they signified an agricultural revival, creating more employment on the land, the local registration officers in all the rural parishes which showed a large increase of population were asked by the census authorities to state to what causes they ascribed it. Of 581 such parishes, only 16 reported that the growth was due to agricultural development, small holdings, fruit farming, market gardening, and the like; in the remaining 565 rural parishes with increased population it was attributed mainly to residential development in the neighbourhood of towns; next, to colliery and manufacturing development, and the erection of public institutions in rural districts; and lastly, to a number of other minor causes in no way connected with agriculture. While, therefore, the detailed census figures, when published, may show some rise in the population engaged in agriculture, this will almost certainly be considerably less than 10 per cent.

The figures given in the table derive additional significance from the fact that the population increases much faster in the large and medium sized towns than in the small towns and urban districts, even though the latter include many

new residential and colliery districts, so that most
of the population which is lost to the countryside
by migration is absorbed by the crowded areas
where conditions of life are least favourable to
the preservation of a high physical standard.

It is unnecessary for us here to dwell on the
serious consequences to the nation of allowing
the rural exodus to continue. These are serious
whether considered from the standpoint of national physique or national character. Stricter
regard to sanitation is slowly improving the
health conditions in urban districts, though a
walk through the poorer quarters of any town in
England shows there will have to be yet more
fundamental changes before the health conditions of cities approach those of rural districts.
An idea of how far they lag behind them at
present may be gained from a comparison of
the death-rates.

Taking the general death-rate, we find that
whereas for rural districts it is $12\frac{1}{2}$ per 1,000
living, in urban districts it is 16.* Or if we take
the mortality in the first twelve months of life,

---

* The figures are the average for the five years 1906 to 1910, and
refer to predominantly rural and urban counties. See Registrar
General's Report, Cd. 5,485, 1911, p. liii.

the figures are 98 per 1,000 children born for rural districts, and 127 for urban districts.

The physique of the town population in the past has been maintained to some extent by constant reinforcement of the anæmic town dwellers by countrymen. But the source from which these reinforcements have been obtained is rapidly becoming exhausted. Already the country dwellers have given up their best, and the prospect, from the point of view of the maintenance of the national physique, is not bright. It is doubtful whether the health conditions in the cities are being improved as rapidly as the vitality of the country districts is being exhausted.

But there is another point of view from which the matter should be considered—that of the national character. Work on the land, in constant contact with natural objects and often in comparative isolation, produces a solid strength of character which our English nation can ill afford to lose. Town dwellers may call the countryman slow or stupid. Certainly he thinks slowly, but his opinions when formed are not infrequently shrewd and sensible, and based on personal observation. The town dweller, on

the other hand, suffers from living too quickly
and living in a crowd. His opinions are the
opinions of the crowd—and a crowd is easily
swayed, for evil as well as for good. Not only,
then, from the point of view of physical deterioration, is it well that at last the British nation has
awakened to the importance of recruiting and
developing her rural districts.

So far we have been concerned with the
reduction in the proportion of rural dwellers
generally. We now pass to a consideration of
the number of agricultural labourers in England
and Wales, and the proportion which these bear
to other sections of agricultural workers. The
census returns of the number of agriculturists
are in all countries very inadequate, and England
is no exception to the rule. In this country,
not only has no satisfactory method of enumerat-
ing the *bonâ fide* agricultural population been
arrived at, but the methods which are employed
vary from census to census—making accurate
deduction impossible. The changes in the mode
of classification between 1871 and 1881 were
so radical that in making comparisons all figures
prior to 1881 must be neglected. From that

date onward it is, however, possible to analyze the figures and bring them into approximate correspondence. The following table is the result of such analysis :—*

	1881.		1891.		1901.	
	Males.	Females.	Males.	Females.	Males.	Females.
Farmers and Graziers	203,329	20,614	201,918	21,692	202,751	21,548
Male relatives of above	75,199	..	67,287	..	89,165	..
Farm Bailiffs . . .	19,377	..	18,205	..	22,623	39
Shepherds	22,844	..	21,573	..	25,354	12
Agricultural Labourers and Farm Servants	807,608	40,346	734,984	24,150	583,751	11,951
Grooms and Coachmen in Rural Districts .	*40,819	44	38,723	..	38,723	..
Gamekeepers . . .	12,633	..	13,814	3	16,677	..
Woodmen	8,151	..	9,448	..	12,034	1
†Gardeners, Nurserymen, Seedsmen, and Florists . . .	145,142	2,409	174,290	5,046	211,025	5,140
†With Agricultural Machines	4,222	38	4,608	67	6,480	65
†Others engaged in Agriculture . . .	6,236	79	5,831	96	5,757	226
Totals . . .	1,345,587	63,530	1,290,681	51,054	1,214,340	38,982
Both Sexes .	1,409,117		1,341,735		1,253,322	

* Including horsekeepers and horsebreakers in 1881.

† These three subdivisions included 10,496 employers in 1891, and 8,683 in 1901. Not distinguished in 18..

The above table shows that, leaving women out of account, the number of agricultural labourers,

* The figures for female relatives of farmers have been omitted because in 1901 only those returned as regularly assisting in farm work were specially enumerated. The number of female farm servants for the three years does not seem reliable, although no doubt there has been a considerable decline. See an article by W. J. Bear in the Journal of the Royal Agricultural Society, Vol. 64, 1903.

farm servants, and shepherds in England and
Wales is a little over 600,000 ; while the total
number of males engaged in agriculture, including
all gardeners, seedsmen, and florists, is just over
1,200,000. Although these are large numbers,
they are not so large as they used to be. Between
1881 and 1901 the number of males engaged in
agriculture in England and Wales decreased by
11 per cent., although the total population
increased during that period by 25 per cent.
During the same period the number of agricultural labourers and male farm servants decreased
by 27·7 per cent. (from 807,608 in 1881 to
583,751 in 1901). In 1881 we had 31 males
engaged in agriculture per square mile of cultivated area in England and Wales; in 1901 the
number was 28. In passing it may be mentioned
that in Belgium the number is 72 per square
mile, and that if the number in England and
Wales were as great as in Belgium nearly two
million more men would be engaged in agriculture
than at present.

There is not the least doubt that the decrease
in the number of agricultural workers, although
partly accounted for by the introduction of

machinery, means that the soil on many farms is not being adequately cultivated. If more workers were employed a greater yield could be obtained, and there is abundant evidence that this could be done at a profit.

The significance of even a comparatively small proportionate increase in the agricultural yield will be at once realized when we remember that the total annual value of the agricultural production of the United Kingdom is estimated at about 210 million pounds.*

It is important to note that 70 per cent. of the agricultural workers in England and Wales are paid labourers, having no direct financial interest in the success or otherwise of the work in which they are engaged, and only 30 per cent. farmers, smallholders, or members of their families. This is a serious fact, for probably in no other European country is there so high a proportion of agricultural workers who are " divorced from the soil."

Moreover, the paid labourer in most Continental countries does not, as a rule, intend to remain a

* See Final Report of First Census of Production, 1907 (Cd. 6,320, 1912).

wage-earner all his life. He intends, when he has saved enough, and when the opportunity occurs, gradually to change his condition for that of an independent smallholder or farmer. However hard his lot may be, *it is only a phase in his life*, and he is always looking forward to becoming his own master.

The fact that in England very few labourers expect to become independent, and that abroad almost all of them expect to do so, is one of supreme importance, and the whole of the facts in this book must be read with the knowledge that they describe not a temporary but a permanent state of things.

One other matter must be dealt with. If, as we have seen, the number of agricultural labourers is much smaller than it was, where have they gone ? The great majority of them have gone into the towns ; an increasing number, however, are leaving England and finding a future in Canada, Australia, or the United States. From the national and agricultural standpoint the most serious consideration is that those who emigrate are the best and most enterprising men, and therefore the quality of the rank and file of agricultural labourers to-day is worse than it was previously, and is steadily deteriorating. Some idea of how rapidly the labourers are leaving the country may be gathered from the fact that the number of adult male agriculturists who emigrated from Great Britain to non-European countries rose from about 9,000 in 1900 to 26,000 in 1907, and, after a fall to 15,000 in 1908, rose steadily to 33,000 in 1911. This means that in 1911 *about one out of every forty agriculturists found his prospects in this country so poor that he decided to quit the country altogether.* We do not know what proportion of those who emigrated were labourers, but from inquiries made at emigration offices, it is evident that the bulk of them belonged to this class

CHAPTER II.

CONSIDERING how exceedingly difficult it is to obtain satisfactory wage statistics, we may congratulate ourselves in this country that very useful figures have been supplied by the Board of Trade. They enable us to state the average wage of agricultural labourers in every county of the United Kingdom in 1907. The figures were obtained by inquiry from farmers, and many labourers claim that they have stated them too high, and that the value of wages paid in kind has been overestimated. Probably we shall be safe in setting off any such overestimate against the slight rise in wages since 1907,* and so may accept the official figures as substantially accurate at the present time.

* See p. 26.

One point, however, must be noted—that the official figures are *county averages*. As a matter of fact, however, there are considerable variations in the wages paid within each county. Of course, the vicinity of an alternative employment, such as is afforded by railways, mines, quarries, or factories, affects the wages of agricultural labourers. But there are often variations in the wages in closely adjacent villages for which there is no apparent cause. Thus in a county where the earnings are given as 16s. they may vary from 14s. in one village to 17s. in a village only a couple of miles away.

After giving these preliminary explanations we may proceed to a consideration of the official figures which will be found in Volume V. of the Report on Earnings and Hours of Labour in 1907 (Cd. 5,460).

In 1907 the weekly earnings of ordinary agricultural labourers in England averaged 17s. 6d. Those of horsemen, cattlemen, and shepherds were a little higher, and if they are included in the general average the figure is raised to 18s. 4d. It should be noted that these figures refer not to cash wages but to *total earnings*, including payment in kind, such, for instance, as free cottage, milk, potatoes, etc., and they take into account all extra payments, such as those for harvest and hay time. It should also be noted that the figures *refer solely to able-bodied male adult labourers in regular employment;* bailiffs, foremen, and stewards are not included, nor are old and infirm men and casual labourers, or women and young persons.

In Wales the weekly earnings for all classes of labourers averaged 18s.—fourpence less than in England. No distinction was made in the Welsh statistics between ordinary labourers and those in charge of animals.

In England about 3s., or nearly one-sixth of the total earnings, represents payment in kind and extra earnings (harvest, hay time, etc.), the remainder being the regular weekly cash wage. In Wales the average weekly cash wage is 13s. 9d., the extra earnings and payment in kind amounting to an average weekly sum of 4s. 3d.

Earnings vary enormously from county to county. To simplify, we may confine ourselves to the earnings of ordinary agricultural labourers.

These vary from 14s. 11d. in Oxfordshire to 20s. 10d. in Derbyshire.* The accompanying map shows that the highest wages are paid in the industrial and mining districts, and the lowest in purely agricultural districts where there are no alternative employments.

We do not propose in this volume to enter in detail into the reasons why wages vary so greatly, or to inquire whether, and if so by what means, wages in the low-paid counties could be raised. It may, however, be noted in passing that there is apparently no difference in the quality of the soil, or in the kind of farming pursued, or in the transit facilities, between the counties with low and with high wages.

It will help us more fully to understand the meaning of the official figures if we classify the agricultural labourers according to the number in each county. We can then ascertain approximately what proportions of the total number fall into the different wage groups. Of course, these figures are not mathematically accurate :

* The wages in Durham and Northumberland are higher—22s. 6d. and 21s. 6d. respectively—but they refer to men in charge of horses ; there are scarcely any labourers in those counties who are not in charge of animals.

firstly, because the census figures refer to 1901 and the wage figure to 1907, and secondly, because, as we have stated above, wages vary greatly within each county; but nevertheless the analysis will give some indication of the proportion of the total number of labourers who are earning different rates of wages.

AGRICULTURAL LABOURERS IN ENGLAND AND WALES (EXCLUDING LONDON), CLASSIFIED ACCORDING TO THE AVERAGE WAGE PA D IN THE COUNTY IN WHICH THEY RESIDE.

Average Wage of County.	Number of Labourers (all classes).	Per Cent. of Total.	Number of Ordinary Labourers.	Per Cent. of Total.
Under 16s	34,113	7·5	34,113	12·6
16s. and under 17s. . .	81,106	17·7	77,287	28·6
17s. and under 18s. . .	97,184	21·2	52,862	19·6
18s. and under 20s. . .	201,770	44·1	101,127	37·5
20s. and over	43,466	9·5	4,598	1·7
Total . . .	457,639	100·0	269,987	100·0

The above table refers only to men who are twenty years of age or over. The figures referring to all classes of labourers have been arrived at by ascertaining from the 1901 census returns the total number of (1) ordinary agricultural labourers, (2) shepherds, (3) horsemen, (4) cattlemen, in each county, and allocating to each group the average weekly earnings in the county (including perquisites) for that particular class of labour, as shown in the Official Report on Wages (Cd. 5,460), which refers to the year 1907.

Before we can attach their true value to these figures, we must ask whether the wages they represent are stationary or advancing rapidly—

whether, in other words, forces are already at work which will automatically bring about a speedy and marked improvement.

Official figures show that the wages of ordinary labourers (excluding those in charge of animals) in England rose from 16s. 9d. in 1898 to 17s. 5d. in 1902, and to 17s. 7d. in 1907.* No figures are given for Wales. It is not possible to go further back than 1898 to obtain general figures, but figures of the wages paid to ordinary labourers on 156 farms in different parts of England and Wales show that, if we take the wages for the year 1900 as equal to 100, they were 92·6 in 1880, remained almost stationary until 1894, when they stood again at 92·6, rose between 1894 and 1900 to 100, since when they have risen to 103·1 in 1910. Later figures are not available. Thus we see that in the last ten years for which statistics are given, there has been a rise of 3 per cent. in the wages of ordinary labourers in England and Wales. But the cost of living has, during that period, advanced by about 10

* The figure differs slightly from that given above—17s. 6d.— because the "weighting" of county average wages had to be recalculated on a different basis, that of the calculations for 1902 in place of that of the calculations for 1898. See Cd. 5,460, p. xiv.

per cent.,* and by a further 5 per cent. between
1910 and 1912, with the result that *the real
wages of agricultural labourers have actually dimin-
ished since* 1900.

NUMBER OF LABOURERS BELOW THE POVERTY LINE.

The meaning of the figures quoted in this
chapter can best be appreciated by comparing
the wages paid with the sum necessary for the
maintenance of a family of average size in
physical efficiency. As one of us has, in a previous
volume,† worked this out in great detail, we need
not here enter into particulars. We shall adopt
the standard set forth in " Poverty," merely
making such modifications as are necessitated
by differences between rural and urban conditions, and the cost of living then and now.
In fixing the amount of nutriment required, the

* All figures showing the rise and fall in the price of foodstuffs
must be regarded as rough estimates only, and the same remark
applies to estimates of general wages based on those paid on so small
a number as 156 farms. But though the figures here given are subject
to some criticism, they confirm the conclusion to which many other
facts point, that real wages have fallen during recent years. See
Board of Trade Gazette, January 1913, p. 4.

† " Poverty : A Study of Town Life," by B. Seebohm Rowntree.
Macmillan, 1901.

standard adopted is that which Prof. Atwater
considers necessary for persons engaged in
" moderate " work, and the dietary selected to
yield the necessary nutriment is more austere
than that provided in any workhouse in England
or Wales. It comprises no butcher's meat, and
only a little bacon ; scarcely any tea, and no
butter or eggs. The cost of all other items of
expenditure is estimated at the very lowest
figure at which physical efficiency can be maintained.

On this basis the weekly minimum for a family
of two adults and three children works out as
follows :—

		s.	*d.*	
Food	. . .	13	9	
Fuel	. . .	1	4	
Rent	. . .	2	0	
Clothing	. .	2	3	(6d. per week for each adult and 5d. per week for each child).
Insurance	. .	0	4	
Sundries	. .	0	10	
		20	6	

It should be noted :—

1. That this estimate allows for no expenditure
on tobacco, beer, newspapers, amusements, railway fares, emergencies, or luxuries of any kind.

2. It assumes much more economical management and knowledge of food values than can be expected from the ordinary working man's wife.

3. The food requirements are based upon Atwater's standard of the nutriment required for persons engaged in " moderate " work, such, for instance, as that of a house painter. There is no doubt that the work of an agricultural labourer is harder than that of a house painter, and consequently it is decidedly within the mark only to allow for the food requirements of a man doing " moderate " work.

4. The cost of foodstuffs has been taken at town prices. As a matter of fact, however, food which has to be bought costs somewhat more in the country than in the town. Mr. F. G. Green, in his book " The Tyranny of the Countryside," * gives figures which support this view, which is also confirmed by Miss Maude E. Davies in "Life in an English Village," † and by Mr. H. H. Mann in "Life in an Agricultural Village in England." ‡ It is, moreover, sufficiently established by the fact that so many thrifty

* T. Fisher Unwin, London, 1913.
† T. Fisher Unwin, London, 1909.
‡ Sociological Papers, Macmillan, 1904.

housewives living in the country will walk miles to buy their meat and groceries in the nearest town.

5. House rent is only taken at 2s. If a commercial rent were to be paid for the cottages, another 2s. would have to be added to this item.

Bearing all these points in mind, *it may be taken as an established fact that a family of five persons whose total income does not exceed 20s. 6d., and whose rent is 2s., is living below the "poverty line."*

We wish to make it perfectly clear that this estimate only allows for expenditure *necessary for the maintenance of physical efficiency.* That a reasonable "living wage" would have to include a further amount for recreation, a more varied dietary, for emergencies, and, generally, to render life less austere, few will deny. But in attempting to estimate how much should be allowed for these purposes we enter a region of controversy where personal opinions must take the place of scientific data. We prefer, therefore, to adopt the above minimum, and merely to state our own strong conviction that such a minimum does not by any means constitute a reasonable living wage.

If we now turn to the actual wages of ordinary agricultural labourers, we find that notwithstanding the fact that we have assumed a poverty line so low as to be open to the criticism of serious inadequacy, yet, with five exceptions (Northumberland, Durham, Westmorland, Lancashire, and Derbyshire), the average earnings in every county of England and Wales are below it.

It is not, of course, suggested that every family is living below this line. Often there are subsidiary earnings by other members of the family which, added to those of the chief wage earner, raise the general level. Often also the number in the family is less than five ; and again, many labourers have gardens or allotments on which they can raise an important proportion of their total food requirements. It would, however, be quite misleading to add the value of the produce so raised to the wage. It is raised by the worker's own labour, in his spare time, upon land for which, directly or indirectly, he pays rent, and it does not affect the conclusions to which we are driven that *the wage paid by farmers to agricultural labourers is, in the vast majority of cases, insufficient to maintain a family of average size in a state of merely physical efficiency.* In considering the question of garden produce, it must further be borne in mind that, according to the official report of the Board of Trade, already quoted (Cd. 5,460), "the hours of labour of ordinary labourers in the summer months are usually 11 or 12 per day, with intervals of $1\frac{1}{2}$ to 2 hours for meals; in a few cases the working time on Saturdays is slightly reduced, but this is not general. In winter the working time is generally limited by the hours of daylight." And, moreover, gardening does not constitute a change of employment, as in the case of the industrial worker, but often is merely a continuation into the late hours of the evening of the work upon which the labourer has been engaged all day.

We have already seen how greatly wages vary within each county. Some are considerably higher, raising the families above the poverty line, although the county average would place them below it. But it must also be remembered that there are *thousands* of agricultural labourers'

families living on total earnings of less than
14s. 11d. a week, which is the lowest county
average.

We have ourselves come across many such,
and have seen enough evidence to be confident
that their number is very considerable.

Mr. C. Roden Buxton, writing in the *Con-
temporary Review* for August 1912, says : " I
have recently been down into Northampton-
shire and Oxfordshire, and I found there that
in many of the villages the wages of the agricultural labourers were 10s., 11s., and 12s. per week,
and they have to lose time in wet weather.
Hundreds of them have gone home at the week-
end during the winter months with only 8s. for
the week. The general statement made to me,
which I can bear out by experience, is that the
average earnings of those labourers do not
amount to more than 12s. per week."

In considering the problem of adequate wages
for a labourer and his family, it has been assumed
that the family will consist of man and wife and
three children. This is, however, in a great many
cases an underestimate. There seems to be more
fatalism, a more complete acceptance of child-

bearing as natural and inevitable, in the country than in the town. The doubtful and dangerous so-called " Malthusian " methods in vogue in towns are less prevalent in the country. And, moreover, the infantile mortality is lower in rural than in urban districts.*

It may be asked, How is it, if so large a proportion of the agricultural labourers are living below the poverty line, that the distress and ill-health among them are not more marked? The answer is that they could not make ends meet at all if it were not for charitable gifts—sometimes of coal, sometimes of food or clothing. It is unnecessary to emphasize the undesirability of this condition of things. It is impossible to raise a virile and independent race under conditions which condemn its members to depend upon charity for their existence.

* Although from the preliminary census returns for 1911 it would appear that the average size of household is almost identical in town and country (namely, 4·4 in the total rural districts, as against 4·5 in the total urban districts), this conclusion is misleading. An analysis of the population figures in the 1901 census (those for 1911 not yet being available) shows that the number of children under fifteen per married woman between the ages of twenty and forty-five is 5 in the rural districts as against 4 in the urban districts, so that we are justified in assuming that the average family of the ordinary agricultural labourer is larger than that of the industrial worker.

It should be further pointed out that the poverty line represents the sum necessary for the maintenance not of mere existence but of physical efficiency. There is not the least doubt that the low-paid labourer who has to maintain a family is not physically efficient. He is a worse all-round man than the well-paid labourer, and he is worse because he does not get enough good food to nourish brain and muscle. It is probably exceptional for him to suffer the actual pangs of hunger. What happens is that the food he eats, while sufficient to allay hunger, does not contain the nutriment necessary for physical efficiency.

CHAPTER III.

BUDGETS.

WE considered the advisability of merely extracting from the notes of visits paid to various families material for a general description of the labourer's life. But we believe that a truer perception of what that life really is will be gained from a perusal of the unembellished records written down with no attempt at literary adornment. They bring one face to face with the hard facts, from which every reader may draw his own conclusions—a much better system of arriving at the truth than reading the conclusions of other people.

One word must be said as to the method by which the information here given was obtained.

When we began our work we tried to get the women to keep actual budgets for a week, putting down each day exactly what was purchased and what was eaten. But a very little experience showed us that the best results could not be thus obtained, and (except for studies Nos. 8, 12, and 33) all the budgets here set forth have been obtained by cross-questioning the housewife as to the way she spent her weekly income, and as to the food consumed at each meal.

In the case of town dwellers, where, except in cases of acute poverty, the variety of food eaten is generally greater, such a method might not give satisfactory results; but in the country the total sum spent weekly is so small, and the dietary varies so slightly from week to week, that the actual facts can be ascertained with great accuracy by this method. Of course for an inquiry undertaken in this way, it is necessary to gain the confidence of the informants, and to continue cross-examination until quite satisfied that complete and accurate facts have been supplied. In certain cases a small sum was paid to the housewife for the trouble taken in supplying information; for a cross-examination, involving, as many of ours did, weighing and examining various foodstuffs, often lasted a considerable time. We may add, however, that practically all the information was given without any thought of or desire for payment.

With three exceptions, all the studies were obtained personally by one of the present writers who visited Yorkshire, Essex, Oxfordshire, Leicestershire, and Berkshire for the purpose. Districts representative of low, medium, and high wages were chosen, and friends living in those districts helped us with introductions or advice as to the most typical villages.

In nearly every case the families selected for investigation were of good reputation for sobriety, thrift, and honesty. Families with an abnormally large number of children were as a rule avoided, but where they occur it will be found that some of the children are working.

It need hardly be added that in conversation the investigator sought to elicit what was in the minds of those spoken to, and not to get them to agree to opinions suggested to them.

In these budgets, the daily bill of fare must be read in conjunction with the amounts of food purchased. A pound of beef, for instance, with a thrifty family may serve three dinners and provide three separate entries—roast beef, cold

beef, and Irish stew, which suggests a liberal
dietary. But when all is said and done, it is
only a pound of beef. Again, one woman will
divide her piece of bacon, at the beginning of
the week, into as many sections as there are
days and reserve it strictly for the man; another
household will live prodigally at the week-end,
and for a great part of the week on bread and
margarine: yet the amount of meat or bacon
consumed may be the same in both cases. It
must also be borne in mind that "roast beef,"
for example, sometimes denotes the cheapest
frozen meat at 4d. a lb.

It will be noted that in the budgets of the
better-off a good deal of pastry is consumed.
Some housewives make nearly half the flour into
pastry. This might seem an extravagance, but
it must be remembered that the pastry is extremely plain and extremely solid. It is usually
regarded by the worker as more satisfying than
bread ; and it saves butter. Though not entered
for breakfast in the menu, we believe that it
sometimes makes its appearance at that meal
also. As a rule, no strict convention is followed
in such things ; it is largely, so long as the

choice remains, a matter of what people fancy, though the thrifty try to " even one day with another."

In the South, where wages are lower, bread is the mainstay; and since good ovens for baking are exceptional, all the bread is bought. The old-fashioned ovens are superseded by small ones, which hold so little at a time that the housewife cannot afford the necessary fuel. They depend largely, however, on " dumplings." But here the reader must not conjure up mentally a rich, flaky substance that melts in the mouth. The dumpling made by a woman with 14s. a week to manage on is substantial; but the suggestion of suet, lard, or dripping it conveys is of the slightest, and if what are technically known as " shouting currants " are present, they may shout, but it is not conceivable that they should be heard !

It will be noted that in hardly any of these budgets is any adequate allowance made for dress. The extent to which even respectable labourers in regular work have in this matter to depend very largely on charity is a grave feature of rural life. It is too readily assumed that overtime money, or Michaelmas money, covers such expenses. But, except in the case of those definitely engaged for six months or a year, overtime money is often more than counter-balanced by the amount of " standing off " in bad weather. And where 30s. or even £2 Michaelmas money is received, it is sometimes required for rent; but even if the cottage is free, such a sum cannot cover clothing for a family for a year.

As for buying on the instalment system—as so many of these people do buy the things that they cannot get given—it inevitably means an unduly high price, and shortage in food.

In these budgets the attempt was made to describe a week that should be typical. The diet, as a rule, varies little all the year round. In the worst times debt is often incurred; in the best times it is paid, or partially paid. Debt, therefore, acts as a leveller of the dietary through-out the year.

It is only necessary to add that the names of persons and villages have been changed, to pre-vent the identification of our informants. The names of the counties are, however, correct.

Study No. I.—Oxfordshire.

Man, wife, three sons, aged eight and a half, six, and one and three-quarters, and one daughter, aged seven.

TOTAL WEEKLY EARNINGS OF FAMILY.

Man's wage . . . . 10s.

Extra earnings in course of the year, 10s., earned by the woman.

Rent of cottage, £2, 15s. per year.

Rent of allotment, 5s. per year.

Mrs. Shaw is a tall, very thin, very worn woman with a pale face full of anxiety. She has to face the winter, and her husband has very little prospect of regular work. Last year they were forced on the parish; but this year, so far, things have looked a little brighter, and November is far advanced. For the last month Mr. Shaw has been averaging 10s. a week, and his wife lives in hope that something may turn up for the winter.

Mr. Shaw is a thoroughly steady fellow, who neither drinks nor smokes, and who bears a good character for industry. But some years ago he

suffered from fits, and though it is three years
and a half since he had one, people are still
unwilling to trust him with a scythe, or with
any work involving the slightest risk. Apart
from that, however, work is scarce in the winter
in this village for all but the hired men. Their
next-door neighbour, who is quite able-bodied,
has had less work than Shaw, though, happily
for him, he has a son working.

Just now Shaw is " sorting potatoes," but
that work will soon be over. Sometimes he has
a couple of days a week as " beater," and then
he gets half a crown and his food.

Mrs. Shaw's sister keeps a small shop in the
village, and though she is not too well off herself, she allows the Shaw family some credit.
They pay her, whenever it is possible, at the end
of the week for the week's provisions ; but if it
is impossible, they try to pay her in the summer.

Mrs. Shaw herself earns a trifle, but only a
few shillings in the year, by " smocking." She
trusts to charity for the children's clothes, and
makes and remakes anything given to her with
great skill. She showed us Percy's suit—made
out of an old pair of trousers—in which the six-

year-old lad looked as neat as possible. She
herself has never had a new dress since her
marriage, though she has been married thirteen
years. There are four children—three boys and
a girl—ranging from nine to two years. In spite
of being so poorly fed, they look clean and happy
and fairly healthy, though less rosy than they
should do. But for the garden, of course, it would
be impossible to live. They have potatoes every
day, greens twice a week. Whenever the funds
run to Quaker oats, they have them for breakfast.

" With milk ? " we asked Mrs. Shaw.

" We can't buy milk. I generally get a tin
of Swiss once a fortnight ; it goes further, and
we only use it in the tea. We haven't had any
new milk in the house for seven years."

Here Lily, the little girl, interrupted eagerly,
" Last year, when I had measles, Mrs. Welch
brought me milk, mum."

" Yes, but that was skim, Lily. I chose skim
because you were so thirsty, and I could get
you more ! "

Mrs. Shaw interviewed us in the bedroom—
or one of the two bedrooms—because the living
room, whenever the wind was from the north,

was full of smoke if a fire were lit. But that was a minor inconvenience; a four-roomed house where rent was only £2, 15s. a year was a veritable godsend. It was certainly dreary; the brick floors downstairs looked extremely comfortless, and one pair of thin blankets for two beds cannot keep out the cold from six people, even when supplemented by all the old clothing in the house.

The light waned as Mrs. Shaw told the story of her difficulties, her contrivances, and their scanty fare. It was evidently the rule not to light the lamp till it was far too dark to see. But there was a curious atmosphere of peace in the place, in spite of its poverty. Somehow or other the woman had managed to keep the working faith in the universe, and in the ultimate purpose of things, that so many more fortunate people miss.

There is a deficiency of 37 per cent. of protein in this family's dietary, and of 20 per cent. of energy value. One-fifth of the food consumed is home produce, and about 4 per cent. is given.*

* The method adopted in this and the following studies for estimating the extent to which the diet is adequate for the maintenance of physical efficiency is explained on p. 300 *et seq.*

EXPENDITURE DURING TYPICAL WEEK IN NOVEMBER 1912.

	s.	d.		s.	d.
1 lb. Quaker oats . . .	0	3	⅛ stone flour	0	3
3 lbs. sugar	0	6	¼ lb. currants . . .	0	1
28 lbs. bread	3	2½	Condensed milk . . .	0	3½
¼ lb. tea	0	4½	1 quart oil	0	2½
2 lbs. margarine . . .	1	0	1 cwt. coal	1	4
5 lbs. brisket beef (frozen)			Insurance	0	3
and ½ lb. suet . . .	2	0	Salt and baking powder	0	1
			Soap, soda, etc. . . .	0	2½
				10	0½

No saving towards rent.

HOME PRODUCE CONSUMED DURING THE WEEK.

38 lbs. potatoes.	1 lb. carrots.
7 lbs. greens.	1 lb. turnips.

GIFTS CONSUMED DURING THE WEEK.

Some bones and scraps of meat which had formerly been used for soup by a neighbour.

	BREAKFAST.	DINNER.	TEA.
SUN. . . .	Tea, bread and margarine, Quaker oats.	Meat, potatoes, greens, small dumpling.	Tea, bread and margarine, currant cake.
MON. . .	Tea, bread and margarine.	Meat, potatoes.	Tea, bread and margarine, cake.
TUES. . .	Tea, bread and margarine, Quaker oats.	Meat, potatoes.	Tea, bread and margarine.
WED. . .	Tea, bread and margarine.	Meat, potatoes, greens.	Tea, bread and margarine.
THUR. . .	Tea, Quaker oats, bread and margarine.	Meat stew, dumplings, onions, potatoes.	Tea, bread and margarine.
FRI. . . .	Tea, bread and margarine.	Remains of stew for man, bread, potatoes.	Tea, bread and margarine.
SAT. . . .	Tea, bread and margarine.	Soup made of bones and scraps, with carrots, turnips, potatoes, parsley.	Tea, bread and margarine.

No supper

Study No. II.—Oxfordshire.

Man, wife, two sons, aged three and six months, and three daughters, aged six, four and a half, and two.

TOTAL WEEKLY EARNINGS OF FAMILY.

Man's wage . . . . 12s.

Extra earnings in course of the year, £1, 8s. (more than counterbalanced by off-time).

Rent of cottage, 1s. 7½d. per week.

Rent of allotment, 1d. per week.

Mrs. Dewhurst is still a young woman, though there are five children, the youngest only an infant. For years she has never been anything but tired; but she has a pleasant face, and must have been an attractive girl. No doubt Dewhurst married her on 12s. a week, hoping that he would soon get a cowman's or horseman's place, or vaguely intending to leave the village. But the years pass, and now to leave would be impossible.

In haytime there is about 4s. a week extra for three weeks, in harvest the same sum for four weeks. But such additional sums are, of course, always mortgaged, especially as in this

village, during the winter, there is a good deal
of standing off—a state of things which the
inhabitants say would be remedied immediately
if half the proper amount of work were put into
the land hereabouts. Last winter " people were
pretty near starved out." Finally, a large land-
owner was appealed to, and he set a number of
men on temporary work.

Dewhurst is a steady, capable fellow who
never touches beer, except when he has a glass
given. Occasionally he earns a newspaper, or
even another ounce of tobacco, by acting as
barber. In his spare time he works on the allotment, for which he pays at the rate of 1d. a week.
The rent runs to 1s. 7½d. a week. The four-
roomed cottage is clean and comfortable, though
perhaps " four-roomed " is too dignified a term.
The second downstairs room is a kind of pantry-
scullery, the second bedroom a landing into
which the stairs open. But there is no lack of
fresh air.

Mrs. Dewhurst's food bill is illuminating.
Three halfpence a week for milk would seem
extravagant, if one did not remember the baby.
The cheap meat—6d. a pound—is, except on

Sundays, when the wife and children have a taste, kept religiously for the breadwinner. Bacon and cheese and eggs are " quite out of the question."

" You can't call it living ; it's a dragging of yourself along," says Mrs. Dewhurst, with a certain amount of quiet bitterness.

" Do you enjoy your food, such as it is ? "

Bread and margarine and potatoes—that is what it is.

" Well, I sometimes think I'd like to sit down and have a real proper dinner."

The allotment, of course, is chiefly laid out with potatoes, as they save bread. But there are summer vegetables, generally used twice a week as long as they last.

Clean as the house is, the look of poverty is unmistakable. Nothing new has been purchased since the Dewhursts became man and wife.

" I've never bought anything new since I married ; but my sisters gave me some black when my father died, and they paid my fare to the funeral."

Mrs. Dewhurst's mother, however, is extremely poor. As she expresses it,—

" It's even more of a lingering with her than
it is with me."

And her sisters have all they can do to help
the mother.

That is the motto of this village : " We don't
live, we linger." It must be remembered that
12s. is the standing wage. But in most of the
families in the neighbourhood the wife or some
grown-up son is working. And young people
are leaving—emigrating, going to towns—rather
than face the problem which Mrs. Dewhurst is
facing—of bringing up a family upon this slender
pittance.

There is a deficiency of 36 per cent. of protein
in this family's dietary, and of 30 per cent. of
energy value. Nearly one-fourth of the food
consumed is home produce.

EXPENDITURE DURING TYPICAL WEEK IN SEPTEMBER 1912.

	s.	d.		s.	d.
¼ lb. tea	0	4½	1 cwt. coal	1	2
26 lbs. bread	2	11¾	¼ stone flour . . .	0	5½
3 lbs. sugar	0	7½	Rent	1	7½
Pepper, salt, and baking			Blacking, hearthstone,		
powder	0	2	boot-laces, matches .	0	3
1 lb. margarine . . .	0	6	Insurance	0	3
Tobacco	0	3½	3 pints separated milk.	0	1½
Soap, soda, and blue .	0	3½			
5 lbs. breast of mutton .	2	6		12	0¼
Oil, candles, and sticks .	0	5			

HOME PRODUCE CONSUMED DURING THE WEEK.

42 lbs. potatoes. | 3 lbs. kidney beans.
3 lbs. parsnips.

MENU OF MEALS PROVIDED DURING THE WEEK.

	BREAKFAST.	DINNER.	TEA.	SUPPER.
SUN..	Tea, bread, fried meat.	Meat pudding, potatoes, kidney beans.	Tea, bread and margarine.	Cold vegetables, bread and margarine.
MON.	Tea, bread and margarine.	Bread and margarine.	Tea, meat (for man), bread, potatoes.	None.
TUES.	Tea, bread and margarine.	Bread and margarine.	Tea, meat (for man), bread, potatoes.	None.
WED..	Tea, bread and margarine.	Bread and margarine.	Tea, meat (for man), bread, potatoes.	None.
THUR.	Tea, bread and margarine.	Bread and margarine.	Tea, meat pudding, bread, potatoes, onions.	None.
FRI. .	Tea, bread and margarine.	Bread and margarine.	Tea, meat (for man), bread, potatoes.	None.
SAT. .	Tea, bread and margarine.	Bread and margarine.	Tea, meat (for man), bread, potatoes.	None.

The man takes bread and margarine with him each day for dinner, having meat and vegetables when he comes home at teatime.

Study No. III.—Oxfordshire.

Man, wife, two sons aged five and three months, and three daughters aged nine, six, and three.

TOTAL WEEKLY EARNINGS OF FAMILY.

Man's wage . . . . 12s.

Extra earnings in course of the year, £1, 6s.
Rent of cottage, 1s. 8d. per week.
Rent of allotment, 14s. 4d. per annum.

Mr. West's regular wage is 12s. Two years ago it came to less, as he lost all wet weather, and, as his wife says, " I couldn't tell you *what* it was like." But at present the 12s. is to be depended upon, and in the summer he makes a little more by piecework. How much more that amounts to is not quite clear. Asked if it raised his wage to 14s. for six months in the year, Mr. West grinned broadly with, " Well, I'm afraid not."

Thirteen shillings for six months would probably roughly represent the facts.

West is a stalwart, well-built man, with a very pleasant, kindly face. His wife says that whatever happens,—

" You'd never hear a word from him in the way of grumbling; he's a Christian man. We've been very happy together, and never had a word amiss ; he just takes things as they come."

Certainly if keeping tranquil and cheery on 12s. a week, with rent to pay and five children to keep, is a test of practical Christianity, West and his wife are both Christians.

Mrs. West, when we began to chat with her, was just busily converting a worn-out pair of men's socks into a pair of boy's socks that should be as good as new. They have endless " shifts and contrivances." Phyllis, the eldest child, sometimes runs an errand and gets a penny. That penny is not spent on sweets, but lodged religiously in the penny bank. By-and-by, pence enough will accumulate there to buy a pair of stockings.

" But how do you live ? "

" I couldn't tell you how we do live ; it's a mystery," with the puzzled look of the poor at the perpetual miracle of continued existence. " I don't know how we manage ; *the thing is to get it past.*"

No victim of satiety and ennui could have said anything stronger ; but the struggle of the Wests to get through the days as they come is really accomplishing something in the way of a home-life, happy in spite of hardship.

In the course of a long conversation we got some light on the way the home was kept going. The ages of the five children range from nine years to three months. The rent is 1s. 8d. per week, paid monthly, for three rooms and a pantry. The rent of their allotment—a quarter of an acre—is 14s. 4d., paid half-yearly. They live largely out of this land, but occasionally West has to lose a day's pay to work on it. His regular hours are, in the winter, from 7 a.m. to 5 p.m., with an hour for dinner; and being a steady, industrious man, he has been working a long while for one master.

Milk is an unusually expensive item in this family, as Mrs. West is not strong enough to nurse her baby, at whose birth she nearly died. That means twopennyworth of milk per day— a pint for 1½d., reserved for the baby, and a third of a pint for the household. Pearl barley must also be bought for the baby—a pound lasting about ten days.

A typical week's budget is given. But some weeks are rather better. For instance, the week before, fourpence had been expended on a pound of liver, which made three dinners for the family.

This cannot always be got, and neither can bones, or probably they would never be without a weekly twopennyworth.

It will be seen that the expenses, even not allowing for extra insurance for the man, or threepence per week insurance for other members of the family, outrun the income. They try to get rid of their debts in the summer. But the fact is that every penny of overtime money should go for clothing. For instance, the man's shoes this year have cost 16s. Clothes for the wife and children are given by the charitable, and altered to serve. But the man's clothes cannot be got in that way; they are bought on the instalment system, and either the food suffers, or there is increased debt. Such debts go on accumulating till one of the children begins to earn.

That the Wests are very little in debt only means that they do not get enough to eat.

There is not much " charity " in the village; but at Christmas nearly 2 cwt. of coal, paid for out of the rent of some land bequeathed to the poor, is given to each of the poorest families. This, of course, signifies that for nearly a fortnight there will be a little more to spend on food, unless the shillings set free are absorbed by debts incurred.

The supply of bread in this budget is given at 20 loaves, sometimes they only have 19. But, taking one week with another, this is typical.

A kindly neighbour whose boys are earning gives Mrs. West the use of her " furnace " on washing-day, making up the fire for her with small coal and potato peelings. This helps to save coal.

There is a deficiency of 30 per cent. of protein in this family's dietary, and of 13 per cent. of energy value. One-eighth of the food consumed is home produce.

EXPENDITURE DURING TYPICAL WEEK IN NOVEMBER 1912.

	s.	d.		s.	d.
40 lbs. bread	4	7	Baking powder, salt,		
¼ stone flour	0	5½	soap, candles, black-		
½ lb. " potted " butter .	0	6	ing, matches . . .	0	1½
9⅓ pints milk	1	2	Faggot of wood . . .	0	2½
⅔ lb. pearl barley . . .	0	2	1 quart oil	0	2½
5 lbs. sugar	0	10	1 cwt. coal	1	3
1 lb. rice	0	2	Insurance	0	3
¼ lb. suet	0	1½	Rent	1	8
2 lbs. bones	0	2			
½ lb. bacon	0	4		12	8¼
⅜ lb. tea	0	6			

HOME PRODUCE CONSUMED DURING THE WEEK.

27 lbs. potatoes.	2 lbs. carrots.
3 lbs. turnips.	5 lbs. greens.

½ lb. onions.

MENU OF MEALS PROVIDED DURING THE WEEK.

	BREAKFAST.	DINNER.	TEA.	SUPPER.
SUN. .	Tea, bread and butter.	Bacon, potatoes, suet pudding, greens.	Tea, bread and butter.	Tea, bread and butter (for two).
MON. .	Tea, bread and butter.	Bacon (for man), potatoes, bread.	Tea, bread and butter.	Tea, bread and butter.
TUES.	Tea, bread and butter.	Bacon, potatoes, bread.	Tea, bread and butter.	Tea and bread.
WED..	Tea, bread and butter.	Soup made of bones, rice, carrots, and turnips; suet dumplings, onions, potatoes.	Tea, bread and butter.	Tea, bread, soup.
THUR.	Tea, bread and butter.	Boiled rice with bones, vegetables.	Tea, bread and butter.	Tea, bread, soup.
FRI. .	Tea, bread and butter.	Suet pudding baked in oven, potatoes, greens.	Tea, bread (butter if any left).	Tea, bread.
SAT. .	Tea, bread and dripping (from bones or meat).	Bread and dripping or sugar, tea.	Tea, bread (butter if any left).	Tea, bread.

The baby is fed on pearl barley and milk (one pint being used each day). Sometimes the man takes with him a piece of bread and butter, or dry bread, to eat between breakfast and dinner.

Study No. IV.—Oxfordshire.

Man, wife, three sons aged five and a half, three, and fifteen months, and one daughter aged eight.

TOTAL WEEKLY EARNINGS OF FAMILY.

Man's wage . . . . 13s.

Extra earnings in course of the year, £2, 12s.

Rent of cottage, 1s. 3d. per week.

Rent of allotment, 4s. per year.

The Leighs seem to be facing the darkness with no immediate hope of the dawn. Robert Leigh is a general labourer earning 13s. a week, as a rule, and 17s. a week, with beer, for three months in the year at the outside. This year he had July, August, and not more than three weeks in September. The more extensive use of machinery in recent years has reduced overtime.

In the winter and spring he works a good deal at digging stones out of some pits which are on the land of his employer. But sometimes the weather makes this impossible.

" I remember one week in December he was four days at home," says his wife. " And in February the pit was flooded; he had three days at home, and then had to ask the master to find him something else to do. We were half hungered to death."

The stones, when dug out of these pits, are sold to neighbouring farmers for road-mending.

This last summer he broke a rib, and was off work for four weeks. This meant 10s. a week from the parish, and an increased burden of debt.

Mrs. Leigh lives in a nightmare. This winter she hopes to pay off a few shillings of debt, because Squire James's coals will be given away at Christmas—6 cwt. to the poorest families—and that will set a little of the wage free, unless, of course, Leigh has to lose time through the weather. But the fact is that for years they have been living a trifle above their income.

" How much do you suppose you owe altogether to all the shops you deal with ?   Ten pounds ? "

" It will be all that—more."

" But how do you manage to get so much credit ?   That's what puzzles one."

" Oh, we have to go where any one will give us a bit of credit. They won't let it run here in the village—I go miles sometimes. And when they worry, we have to pay a bit off and go short. It isn't as if we were extravagant. I've had no new clothes since I've been married. One of the children is off school to-day for want of a pair of shoes."

She was obviously a respectable, honest, hard-working woman. The room was neatly kept, though very poor. But she looked simply weighed down with care. It was written on her face that she could not pay her way.

" I sleep all right till about twelve," she said, " and then I wake and begin worrying about what I owe, and how to get things. Last night I lay and cried for a couple of hours."

The last doctor's fee of a guinea is not paid, and she is expecting another child. Again, they only pay 1s. 3d. rent, but their garden is very small. Their allotment is also small : allotments are rather dear in this village. They have—in the latter end of November—only three or four boilings of greens, a few turnips and parsnips, and a bushel of potatoes left.

Possibly greater knowledge of food values might enable Mrs. Leigh to get more nourishment out of her weekly expenditure ; still, one can hardly call it luxurious or extravagant. The coal bill could hardly be reduced ; for a woman with a young family, in a comfortless, draughty cottage, when washing-day comes once a week, $1\frac{1}{2}$ cwt. is little enough. Perhaps now and then they pick up wood enough to spare the weekly "faggot," but this is more likely to happen when the children are rather older. The budget allows nothing whatever for expenses of clothing, and nothing for paying off debts. In respect of debt, such people become so utterly despondent that they go on sinking lower and lower into the mire, as long as tradespeople will allow them to do so. The outlook is sufficiently depressing, and the winter has only just begun.

There is a deficiency of 39 per cent. of protein in this family's dietary, and of 21 per cent. of energy value. One-tenth of the food consumed is home produce.

EXPENDITURE DURING TYPICAL WEEK IN NOVEMBER 1912.

	s.	d.		s.	d.
24 lbs. bread	2	9	1½ cwt. coal	1	10½
½ stone flour	0	11	Insurance	0	3
1 lb. lard	0	7	Soap, soda, blacking,		
½ lb. butter	0	7½	salt, etc.	0	3½
¼ lb. cocoa	0	2	Oil and candles	0	3
1¼ lbs. bacon	1	0	1 oz. tobacco	0	3½
2½ lbs. pork	1	8	Wood	0	2
3 pints separated milk	0	1½	3 lbs. sugar	0	6
½ lb. suet	0	3			
¼ lb. tea	0	4½		13	4
Rent	1	3			

HOME PRODUCE CONSUMED DURING THE WEEK.

16½ lbs. potatoes. | 4 lbs. turnips.
5 lbs. greens.

MENU OF MEALS PROVIDED DURING THE WEEK.

	BREAKFAST.	DINNER.	TEA.	SUPPER.
SUN. .	Tea, bread and butter or lard.	Roast meat, suet pudding, potatoes, greens, turnips.	Tea, bread and butter, cake.	Bread and butter, cocoa.
MON.	Tea, bread and butter or lard.	Vegetables and pudding fried up.	Tea, bread and butter or lard. (Man has vegetables warmed.)	Bread and butter, cocoa.
TUES.	Tea, bread and butter or lard.	Bread and butter. (Washing day.)	Tea, bread and butter or lard.	Bread and butter, cocoa.
WED..	Tea, bread and butter or lard.	Potatoes, bread and butter or lard.	Tea, bread and butter or lard. (Man has potatoes.)	Bread and butter, cocoa.
THUR.	Tea, bread and lard or butter.	Suet pudding, potatoes, greens.	Tea, bread and lard. (Man has vegetables and pudding.)	Bread and butter, tea.
FRI. .	Tea, bread and lard or butter.	Rest of suet pudding, potatoes, boiled bacon.	Tea, bread and butter or lard. (Man has a little bacon and vegetables.)	Bread and butter, tea.
SAT. .	Tea, bread and butter or lard.	Bread and scrape, tea.	Tea, bread and lard.	Bread and lard, tea.

One in the family only has supper (woman).

Leigh takes his dinner with him to work. This consists of a little beef or bacon, bread and butter or lard, cocoa or tea.

Study No. V.—Oxfordshire.

Man, wife, one son aged six, and two daughters aged eight and three.

TOTAL WEEKLY EARNINGS OF FAMILY.

Wage—		*s.*	*d.*
Man		13	0
Wife		0	4½
		13	4½

Extra earnings in course of the year, £3.
Rent of cottage, 1s. 3d. per week.
Rent of allotment, £1, 10s. per year.

The Allens are a cheery, plucky family. When the interviewer called on them, it was dinner-time; but Mrs. Allen had just finished, so she could talk. Her father, a hale old man of over seventy, with a fresh colour and a benignant expression, was sitting at the table finishing his meal. Her husband had taken lunch with him, and would not be back till teatime. The old man generally comes to dinner two or three times a week, as he has no one at home to look after him, and on these occasions he generally brings a " bit of bacon " with him to replenish the Allen larder—not more, however, than half a pound or a pound in the week at the out-side.

Asked whether they thought that the current standing wage of 13s. was enough, the Allens were unanimous.

" We don't *think* nothing about it; we *know* 'tain't ! "

The old man added,—

" Everything's dear except hard work, and you can have as much as you like of that, cheap ! "

Pressed to explain how she spent her 13s. weekly, Mrs. Allen began to enumerate the various items. We soon found that we had got up to 15s. 6d., and the old man observed, in a satisfied manner,—

" I thought you was putting down more than you had ! "

" But perhaps you *do* spend more than you have ? "

" No, we keep in the 13s., unless we get into debt; and when you get in you have to get out "—a statement that might have been con-tested.

So we began again, and thrashed the subject

out. Mrs. Allen's neighbour, a tall, handsome
woman, whose own husband was earning 15s. a
week, and who had a daughter working, came in
and assisted. She gave it as her opinion that
for a labourer's wife with a young family to
get into debt was " not a sin." This was a generous statement, as she herself had tried to keep
a little shop, and had been compelled to give up
because of bad debts.

The Allens have a large allotment—19 chains
—for which they pay 30s. a year. Their potatoes
last from the beginning of August to the end of
March, or about eight months in the year. This
year they dug up seven sacks.

When the husband works overtime, at harvest
and haymaking, his master offers him the choice
between beer and beer money, and as he chooses
the money his wage amounts to 19s. weekly for
about ten weeks in the year.

" We never seem to be any better off for it,"
they say. The rent of the allotment, clothing,
and any inevitable expenses that arise during
the year have to be met out of this " summer
money."

Mrs. Allen's father remarked with a chuckle

that some time ago he had a woman who had formerly been in the workhouse to look after him. He has the pension, and sometimes earns a little as well. But, he continued,—

" The old gal said she was used to a change of diet where she'd been. She didn't like *my* diet. They live better in the workhouse than we do here."

There is a deficiency of 26 per cent. of protein in this family's dietary, and of 7 per cent. of energy value. One-sixth of the food consumed is home produce, and 2 per cent. is given.

EXPENDITURE DURING TYPICAL WEEK IN NOVEMBER 1912.

	s.	d.		s.	d.
5¼ lbs. flour	0	8	Rent of cottage (3		
26 lbs. bread	3	0	rooms)	1	3
3 lbs. pudding beef . .	1	6	Oil and candles . . .	0	3½
¾ lb. currants	0	3	1½ cwt. of coal . . .	1	10½
½ lb. lard (cooking) . .	0	3½	Insurance	0	3
½ lb. tea	0	9			
5 lbs. sugar	0	10		13	1
1 lb. butter	1	3	Balance towards clothing	0	3½
½ lb. suet	0	3			
3 pints new milk . . .	0	4½		13	4½
4 bloaters	0	3			

HOME PRODUCE CONSUMED DURING THE WEEK.

35 lbs. potatoes.	3 lbs. turnips.
3 lbs. sprouts.	3 lbs. parsnips.

4 oz. onions.

GIFT CONSUMED DURING THE WEEK.

1 lb. bacon.

MENU OF MEALS PROVIDED DURING THE WEEK.

	BREAKFAST.	DINNER.	TEA.	SUPPER.
SUN. .	Tea, bread and butter.	Gravy pudding, potatoes, greens, tea.	Tea, cake with currants, bread and butter.	Tea, bread and butter.
MON. .	Tea, bread and butter.	Bloaters, potatoes, tea (man takes meat and bread with him).	Tea, bread and butter (bloater and potatoes for man).	None.
TUES.	Tea, bread and butter.	Broth (made with meat and onions), potatoes (man takes bread with him).	Tea, bread and butter (man has meat out of broth and potatoes).	None.
WED..	Tea, bread and butter.	Suet pudding with currants, bacon, potatoes, swedes (man takes bread and butter with him).	Tea, bread and butter (man has bacon and vegetables).	None.
THUR.	Tea, bread and butter.	Currant dumpling, bacon, bread (man takes bread and scrap of bacon with him).	Tea, bread and butter (man has dumpling and scrap of bacon).	None.
FRI. .	Tea, bread and butter.	Suet pudding with currants, potatoes, parsnips (man takes bread and butter with him).	Tea, bread and butter (man has vegetables and pudding).	None.
SAT. .	Tea, bread and butter.	Bread and butter, tea (man takes bread and butter with him).	Tea, bread and butter.	None.

Study No. VI.—Berkshire.

Man, wife, two sons aged five and three and a half, and two daughters aged two and seven months.

TOTAL WEEKLY EARNINGS OF FAMILY.

	s.	d.
Man's wage	12	0
Perquisites—		
Cottage and garden, say	2	0
	14	0

Extra earnings in the course of the year, 15s.

The Carrs are people who hitherto have just managed to pay their way. Carr has 12s. weekly and his cottage, and there are four children under school age. Probably they have not yet come to the period of most acute stress, but things are quite difficult enough.

The pint of milk a day sent by the one Lady Bountiful of this neighbourhood—not herself rich—makes a good deal of difference. And most of the clothes are given.

" I have big things given, and make little ones out of them," says Mrs. Carr.

Of course there is always the problem of shoes

and clothes for the man, who gets very little overtime. He is a general labourer, but has to go twice on Sunday—for about $2\frac{1}{2}$ hours altogether—to look after the horses or cattle. He is a sturdy, capable-looking fellow, with a deeply-rooted distrust of politics and politicians.

" I read the paper," he says, " and my father read it before me—and they'll never *do* anything. They promise before the election, but it's a different thing afterwards."

He thinks that it is absolutely impossible to get the labourers to combine when their living is so precarious, and so many men are ready to fill the place of a man who " stands out."

And he is quite sure that the wealthier classes, like the politicians, will " never do anything useful." In short, he is a pessimist, but a hard-working, peaceful pessimist. His luxury is an ounce of tobacco—Navy cut—every week. He never touches beer ; and in his spare time he works hard at the garden, with the sage reflection that many people are worse off than himself.

With care, they make the potatoes last the whole year round, though they could easily use more ; and they have greens and other vegetables for some months as well. Carr gave 15s. as the outside estimate of what he had earned by overtime this year.

There is a deficiency of 29 per cent. of protein in this family's dietary, and of 11 per cent. of energy value. Nearly 10 per cent. of the food consumed was home produce, and 6 per cent. was given.

EXPENDITURE DURING TYPICAL WEEK IN NOVEMBER 1912.

	s.	d.		s.	d.
3½ lbs. fresh beef (brisket)	1	9	Soap and soda	0	2½
28 lbs. bread	3	2½	1 oz. tobacco	0	4½
¼ stone flour	0	5½	Insurance (for all the		
1½ lbs. dripping (1 lb. su-			family)	0	9
perior and ½ lb. inferior			Weekly newspaper	0	1
quality)	0	10			
1 lb. rice	0	2		11	5
¼ lb. tea	0	4			
6 lbs. sugar	1	0	Balance towards shoes,		
1 lb. oatmeal	0	2	clothes, and household		
½ lb. cheese	0	4½	sundries	0	7
1 cwt. coal	1	3			
Wood	0	2		12	0
1 quart oil, candles and					
matches	0	3½			

HOME PRODUCE CONSUMED DURING THE WEEK.

12 lbs. potatoes.	2 lbs. turnips.
2½ lbs. savoys.	2 lbs. parsnips.
5½ lbs. sprouts.	1 lb. onions.

GIFT CONSUMED DURING THE WEEK.
7 pints new milk.

MENU OF MEALS PROVIDED DURING THE WEEK.

	BREAKFAST.	DINNER.	TEA.
SUN. . . .	Bread and drip-ping, porridge, milk, tea.	Roast meat, baked potatoes, pudding, made with flour, dripping, etc.	Tea, bread and dripping.
MON. . . .	Bread and milk, bread and drip-ping, tea.	Sunday's pud-ding fried up, meat, greens, potatoes.	Tea, bread and dripping.
TUES. . . .	Bread and drip-ping, porridge, tea.	Meat, boiled rice, potatoes, vegetables.	Tea, bread and dripping.
WED. . . .	Bread and milk, bread and drip-ping, tea.	Stewed meat, onions, rice, po-tatoes, and par-snips.	Tea, bread and dripping.
THUR. . .	Bread and drip-ping, porridge, tea.	Meat pudding (with remain-der of meat), potatoes.	Tea, bread and dripping.
FRI. . . .	Bread and su-gar, bread and milk, tea.	Boiled dump-lings, bread, potatoes.	Tea, bread and dripping.
SAT. . . .	Bread, porridge, tea.	Boiled rice (with sugar), bread.	Tea, bread and sugar.

The man takes a piece of bread and cheese to eat between breakfast and dinner.

No supper, as a rule, but on Saturday night the man sometimes has a drink of tea on his return from shopping.

Study No. VII.—Berkshire.

Man, wife, one son aged ten, and five daughters aged twelve, eight, seven, five, and fourteen months.

TOTAL WEEKLY EARNINGS OF FAMILY.

	s.	*d.*
Man's wage	12	0
Perquisites—		
Cottage and garden, say . . .	2	0
	14	0

Extra earnings in the course of the year, £2.

Mrs. Bell is a buxom, open-faced woman, cheery and energetic, capable on occasion probably of giving people " the dark side of her tongue."

There are eight at home, including father and mother. The eldest girl—fourteen—is now away in service, and self-supporting. They make their living room of what is really the back room, since the other, though large and pleasant, is very cold, and requires more fuel in winter. As it is, they use 2 cwt. of coal a week in the winter months. The man goes to work at 4.30, and comes back to breakfast at 6, and a fire is burning from about 5 a.m. to 8 p.m., by which time

3 *a*

the family is generally in bed. Washing-day, too, requires a good deal of fuel when there are eight to wash for, and all the villagers are very particular about having the children neat, clean, and " like other children."

At present they are only cooking potatoes three times a week, at the rate of $4\frac{1}{2}$ lbs. a day, that they may last for a good part of the winter, though even so they will hardly see January out. Then either there will be potatoes to buy or more bread. Of greens they had a great many in the summer ; and at present they are cooking carrots, parsnips, or cabbages twice a week. Perhaps these vegetables thus used will last till Christmas.

They will not touch their " seed potatoes." That would mean buying more, and they cannot afford it. Possibly with more work put into it the garden—a large one—might yield more ; but, considering the hours many of these men work already, the wonder is that they spend as much time as they do on their own land, patiently digging or planting till it is almost too dark to see. Of course, they know that if they did not they would positively starve.

There is Sunday work. The man goes twice a day for three or four hours altogether. There is an hour for dinner, and an indefinite time for breakfast, sometimes half an hour, sometimes three-quarters of an hour, sometimes only twenty minutes, as,—

" If they loses their cattle they has to go and find them."

Mrs. Bell sorely grudges the ounce of tobacco consumed nearly every week by her husband. But he always contends, " If I didn't have that, I should want more food!" which seems to settle the question.

The value of jam is another debatable point. It is certainly good for the children; but Mrs. Bell never buys it as a substitute for margarine, for the following reason :—

" If they eat jam, it includes more bread— they eats more! If I cut a slice of bread and put margarine on it, may be two slices will do; but if I put jam on it, it'll be, ' Mummy, give me another slice.' That's my conclusion about jam."

Her views are very pronounced about a good many other things.

" People think we're well off because we've the house free. What I say to 'em is, ' We can't eat the house.' "

She thinks that " so many children are allotted to every one "—one way of meeting the Malthusian problem. She also has a theology of her own, which she finds comforting. In speaking of an old gentleman who used to drive past —a wealthy, but not very generous person—she remarked,—

" And when he went past I always said, ' Ah, old man, when you die, you won't take anything with you—only yourself.' And he *is* dead ; and," with deep satisfaction, " he could only take himself. He left all his money behind him ! But I think," she added, " them that have the least now will have the most then. We've got hell here, *we* have ; *we* shall get something good ! But I believe hell's their place what don't look after the poor."

And Mrs. Bell beamed with exultation. Her faith in immortality is unquestioning and childlike, and she evidently looks forward keenly to getting even with a good many people in the future life.

Meanwhile the real trouble in this household is debt. To be sure, there are natural longings for something different in the way of food, " something noice." One gets weary of buying " the meanest you can " in every department. But that grievance would be nothing if one could pay one's way.

" I'd rather go without myself than be owing," says Mrs. Bell ; " but when the children haven't enough, you have to try to get it where you can. And the last baby cost 9s., and 6s. for a woman, and 2s. for washing, and everything went to ruin."

There is a little debt perhaps at half a dozen shops, including those represented by the men who come round. It cannot be a great deal, but it means endless worry. People are naturally reticent about those things, but I imagine that the debts incurred by the Bells, chiefly for bread, partly for shoes and boots, must amount to £4 or £5.

The coal, too, is a problem. They generally buy it half a ton at a time ; but just now the farmer is going to buy them a ton, which they will pay for when Mr. Bell is earning rather more. Then at Christmas a charity belonging to the parish gives several hundredweights of coal to the poorest families, so that coal money will for a time be liberated for the payment of debts. Mrs. Bell calculated, however, that all the extra money earned by the man did not amount to more than £2 in the year. So one can see what a perpetual struggle life is.

Clothes are, in the main, a matter of charity. One lady in the village gives Mrs. Bell a good many old clothes, and also a pint of milk a day. They need new blankets badly; but to buy a pair by instalments would mean a drain of a shilling per week on the exchequer during these months when least food from the garden is available.

" If you don't pay the shilling, I'll fetch back the blankets," says the salesman ; and the result is that the blankets are not bought.

The budget shows a slight excess of expenditure over income, which must not be allowed to continue. The saved coal money, which ought to mean additional food, will have to wipe off this and some back debts as well, not to mention shoes, which are a constant drain. And it will be clear that any relief of the stress is only obtained through charity.

The tea seems extravagant—$\frac{1}{2}$ lb. ; but they use it at every meal. The man takes no beer, and now that fewer vegetables are being used, and that winter has come, they all like " a warm drink."

There is a deficiency of 34 per cent. of protein in this family's dietary, and of 20 per cent. of energy value. One-thirteenth of the food consumed is home produce, and one-twentieth is a gift.

EXPENDITURE DURING TYPICAL WEEK IN NOVEMBER 1912.

	s.	d.		s.	d.
48 lbs. bread	5	6	Oil and candles . . .	0	4
¼ stone flour	0	5½	Tobacco	0	3½
6 lbs. sugar	1	0	Insurance	0	3
3 lbs. chilled mutton . .	1	0			
2 lbs. margarine . . .	1	0		12	7
2 cwt. coal	2	6			
Soap, soda, blue . . .	0	3			

HOME PRODUCE CONSUMED DURING THE WEEK.

18 lbs. potatoes.	2 lbs. carrots.
4 lbs. savoys.	2 lbs. parsnips.

GIFT CONSUMED DURING THE WEEK.

7 pints new milk

Menu of Meals provided during the Week.

	BREAKFAST.	DINNER.	TEA.
SUN. . . .	Bread and margarine, tea.	Mutton, greens and potatoes, tea.	Tea, bread and margarine.
MON. . . .	Bread and margarine, tea.	Bread and margarine, tea (washing-day, so nothing cooked).	Tea, bread and margarine.
TUES. . . .	Bread and margarine, tea.	Meat (for man), potatoes, boiled pudding, tea (pudding made with flour and fat or margarine).	Tea, bread and margarine.
WED. . . .	Bread and margarine, tea.	Meat (for man), bread and margarine, tea.	Tea, bread and margarine.
THUR. . .	Bread and margarine, tea.	Meat (for man), potatoes, parsnips, carrots, tea.	Tea, bread and margarine.
FRI. . . .	Bread and sugar, tea.	Meat (for man), potatoes, dumplings, tea.	Tea, bread and sugar.
SAT . . .	Bread and sugar, tea.	Bread and margarine, scrap of meat (for man), tea.	Tea, bread and margarine.

No supper. The pint of milk which is given daily is mainly used for the baby.

Study No. VIII.—Bedfordshire.

Man, wife, three sons aged ten, eight, and seven, and three daughters aged thirteen, five, and two.

TOTAL WEEKLY EARNINGS OF FAMILY.

Man's wage . . . . 14s.

Rent of cottage and garden, 1s. 8d. per week.
Rent of allotment, 6s. 6d. per year.
No extra earnings.

Though at present Mr. Barrington is working at a rural lime-kiln and not on the land, we have included the budget of the household, since he receives the normal rural labourer's wage, even to the extent of being docked in wet weather. There are no perquisites and there is no over-time, as the " works " have been slack for some years.

It is a poor village, in which the only charities are for the occupants of cottages under a par-ticular landlord, or the attendants at a particular place of worship, and the Barringtons do not belong to either of these classes. They are now a little better off than they were, by virtue of the allotment which they have begun to rent—

a rood, at 6s. 6d. yearly.   The soil is productive,
and will supply a good many vegetables.

In spite of this the nourishment is terribly
inadequate.   The school doctor visited the family
recently to complain that the children, though
clean and evidently well cared for, were underfed; but when he heard the amount of the
income, he could only say, " Poor souls ! "

The remark, taken in connection with the
abnormally low amount of nutritive value which
this family obtains, reminded us of the words of
a woman living in the same district.   She was
speaking of a former neighbour, who had faced
the Barrington problem on the Barrington wage.

" And how did she manage ? " we asked.

" Oh, she died ! "

The family under review seems to be on the
way to a similar solution of the problem.

There is a deficiency of 49 per cent. of protein
in this family's dietary, and of 42 per cent. of
energy value.   One-seventh of the food consumed
is home produce.

EXPENDITURE DURING TYPICAL WEEK IN OCTOBER 1912.

	s.	d.		s.	d.
7 oz. tea	0	8¾	1½ cwt. coal	1	10½
3 lbs. sugar	0	6¾	1 quart oil and candles .	0	3½
14 oz. lard	0	8¾	Washing materials, black		
¼ lb. butter	0	4	lead, laces, etc. . .	0	6
31 lbs. bread	3	6	Insurance	0	3
4 lbs. flank beef . . .	2	0			
½ gallon skimmed milk .	0	3½		13	6¾
1 lb. oatmeal	0	3	Balance towards shoes		
1 bottle ginger ale . .	0	1	and clothing . . .	0	5¼
1 lb. rice	0	2			
1 lb. jam	0	4		14	0
Rent	1	8			

HOME PRODUCE CONSUMED DURING THE WEEK.

30 lbs. potatoes.	2 lbs. parsnips.
4 lbs. cabbage.	1½ lbs. onions.

GIFT CONSUMED DURING THE WEEK.

1 lb. golden syrup.

Menu of Meals provided during the Week.

	BREAKFAST.	DINNER.	TEA.	SUPPER.
SUN.	Bread and lard, tea.	Meat, potatoes, cabbage.	Tea, bread and butter.	Bread and lard, tea.
MON.	Meat and bread (for man), bread and lard, tea.	Potatoes, parsnips.	Tea, bread and lard.	Bread and lard, tea.
TUES.	Meat and bread (for man), bread and lard, tea.	Potatoes, cabbage.	Tea, bread and syrup.	Bread and lard, tea.
WED.	Meat and bread (for man), porridge, tea.	Potatoes, broth.	Tea, bread and syrup.	Bread and lard, ginger ale.
THUR.	Meat and bread (for man), bread and lard, tea.	Rice, jam.	Tea, bread and lard.	Porridge.
FRI.	Meat and bread (for man), bread and lard, tea.	Meat, potatoes, parsnips, onions.	Tea, bread and jam.	Rice, bread and syrup, tea.
SAT.	Meat and bread (for man), bread and lard, tea.	Meat and bread.	Tea, bread and jam.	Bread and lard, tea.

Study No. IX.—Essex.

Man, wife, one son aged five, and two daughters aged three and one.

TOTAL WEEKLY EARNINGS OF FAMILY.

Man's wage . . . . 15s.

Extra earnings in course of the year, £2, 12s. (man, £2 ; woman, 12s.). Counterbalanced by off-time.

Rent of cottage, £6 per year.

The Burtons are people who, one feels strongly, ought to be in a more stable economic position. They are both, by birth and training, built for respectable security, and insecurity wears them out. Harry Burton, a thoroughly wholesome, industrious young fellow (for he is still young), is the son of an old gamekeeper, a trusted servant on the estate of a very wealthy man. About ten years ago he married a woman three years older than himself, who had proved extremely competent in " service," and was fitted in every way to be a good wife and mother. He was in regular work when they married, and they had saved enough to furnish the house nicely and make a fair start.

The prospect was as rosy as that of an agricultural labourer on 15s. a week could be, but there came illness. Harry Burton was laid aside for months, and lost his regular work. They passed through great straits, and every valuable belonging to the wife was sold, while the house began to look bare and comfortless. Luckily, old Mr. and Mrs. Burton, who live in the village, did all they could; but for them the young couple would possibly have been forced into the workhouse. A woman with a baby and a sick husband to look after cannot go out to work. As it was, they pulled through; and Harry Burton got back to work again, though his work has never since been absolutely regular. He is a day labourer merely, and they often suffer acutely from the incidence of " off-time," even though they are in a better position than many people, inasmuch as old Mr. Burton, the gamekeeper, uses all his influence to get Harry some work on the estate when things are very bad.

The annual rent of the four-roomed cottage is heavy—£6—paid every January. They never try to set aside any money weekly towards this sum, relying upon harvest money and the sale of garden produce. Fortunately, they have an excellent garden, which, while the children are young, supplies them with vegetables for the greater part of the year, and yields a margin for profit—in cabbages, lettuce, onions, etc. They have occasionally to buy potatoes.

Harry Burton gives his wife 12s. out of his 15s. when he has a full week, reserving 3s. for his own clothing, club, insurance, and other personal expenses. He does not smoke, but takes a glass of beer now and then.

The harvest money comes to about £2. Sometimes Mrs. Burton earns a little by field work. This summer she took the children with her, and earned 12s. by picking potatoes. With this she bought boots for the boy and girl, slippers for the boy, socks and stockings for herself and the children, and had her own shoes mended. She would have worked another eight days for another 12s., but the baby's illness prevented it.

The three children are well cared for, and are commonly called " lovely children." But the youngest is distinctly less healthy than the other two. And one close friend of the family, who has helped them in various ways, says that they have lost something in these years of stress and anxiety, some ideal of daintiness—no other word could be found to characterize the exquisite neatness of the Burton menage for some years after they married, or their punctilious care for the first baby when it came. It might have been born in the purple!

But doubtless some ideals have to go in this rough-and-tumble world, and the Burtons have kept their share in honesty, industry, and affection.

There is a deficiency of 7 per cent. of protein in this family's dietary, and of 5 per cent. of energy value. One quarter of the food consumed is home produce.

Expenditure during Typical Week in September 1912.

	s.	d.		s.	d.
¼ lb. currants	0	1	1 lb. liver	0	4
¼ lb. tea	0	4½	⅓ lb. suet	0	2
4 lbs. sugar	0	10	½ lb. dripping	0	2½
¼ lb. cocoa	0	4	1¼ lbs. fresh herrings	0	3
2 lbs. Quaker oats	0	6	1 quart oil	0	3
1 lb. cheese	0	9	Clothing club	0	2
½ lb. rice	0	1¼	Soap, matches	0	3
½ cwt. coal	0	8			
7 pints new milk	1	2		12	0¼
16 lbs. bread	2	0			
¼ stone flour, and 1d. baking powder	0	6½	Man's pocket money for clothing, insurance, club, etc.	3	0
½ lb. butter	0	6			
½ lb. lard	0	3½		15	0¼
3 lbs. steak	2	3			

14 lbs. potatoes. | 1½ lbs. apples.
4 lbs. beans. | 2 lbs. jam.

MENU OF MEALS PROVIDED DURING THE WEEK.

	BREAKFAST.	DINNER.	TEA.
SUN. . . .	Tea, porridge, bread and butter or dripping.	Beef, potatoes, beans, apple tart, cocoa.	Tea, bread and jam, cake (with lard and currants), cheese.
MON. . . .	Tea, porridge, bread and dripping.	Cold meat, potatoes, bread and butter, cocoa.	Tea, bread and jam, cheese.
TUES.. . .	Tea, porridge, bread and butter.	Meat warmed up, beans, potatoes, rice pudding, cocoa.	Tea, bread and jam, cheese.
WED. . . .	Tea, porridge, bread and dripping.	Suet pudding with currants, potatoes, cocoa.	Tea, bread and jam, cheese.
THUR. . .	Tea, porridge, bread and butter.	Liver, potatoes, bread pudding, cocoa.	Tea, bread and jam, cheese.
FRI. . . .	Tea, porridge, bread and butter or dripping.	Fish, potatoes, suet pudding, cocoa.	Tea, bread and jam or butter.
SAT. . . .	Tea, porridge, bread and butter or dripping.	Rice pudding, bread and butter or dripping or jam, cocoa.	Tea, bread and jam or butter.

No supper.

Study No. X.—Essex.

Man, wife, two sons aged thirteen and eleven,
and three daughters aged nine, seven, and three.

TOTAL WEEKLY EARNINGS OF FAMILY.

Man's wage . . . . 15s.

Extra earnings in the course of the year, £2, 7s.,
earned by the woman.

Rent of cottage, 2s. per week.

The Latimers are of a more nervous type than
the average labourer and his wife. They are
both slightly built ; she is dark, with an eager,
mobile face ; he is fair, and looks at present
somewhat below par. He has been working
nearly seven years for Mr. X., who is, on the
whole, a good master, though his wages are not
high—15s. a week, out of which 2s. must go for
rent.

Formerly Latimer was a cowman, but the
long hours—always starting work at 4 a.m.—
and the constant work, with never a Sunday
off, were probably too much for him. At all
events, after a sharp attack of pneumonia which
nearly cost him his life, he became a day labourer.

Now his hours are 7 a.m. to 5 p.m. in the winter, and 6 a.m. to 5.30 p.m. in the summer.

Before the pneumonia, his wife told us, he was as strong as any man, but it left behind some weakness. Last year he was off for six weeks with eczema. They were in no club, and had to resort to the parish, which granted them 6s. weekly—for man and wife and six children. She said it had been impossible to pay into a club. His master, on being appealed to, supplemented the relief with 5s. weekly, and somehow or other they pulled through without getting into debt to any extent.

Latimer is working steadily again now; he is a capable, conscientious fellow. They live in half of what was originally a farm house, a picturesque place. But the interior, though the walls are covered with almanacs and cheap pictures—and it has all the little knick-knacks that give a workman's cottage a look of home— is dreary, simply because the fire is far too meagre for a raw December day.

They pay into a coal club at the rate of 16s. 6d. yearly, and for this they get a ton of coal. The wood is given, and by using some wood they contrive to make the one ton last a year. But a couple of loads of wood a year and a ton of coal, with probably some wood picked up, evidently do not run to cheerful fires.

The garden is not large, and only supplies potatoes for two months in the year. But they have had a good many greens and parsnips, and just at present are using more of these than of potatoes. There are no fruit trees, and this year Mrs. Latimer has made 42 lbs. of jam out of blackberries and apples.

" Where did you get the apples ? "

" I begged them ! "

They were windfalls probably, but served their purpose—to supply jam for the winter. At present she is using a 3-lb. jar a week. She made 10s. this autumn by selling blackberries at 1s. a peck ; and that sum, or part of it, helped with the sugar for boiling her own jam. She also paid up arrears with the coal club.

Other small alleviations in the lot of the Latimer family are 7 lbs. of beef and a couple of rabbits at Christmas from the employer—the latter given to all his tenants, the first only to his labourers. But during the shooting season they get a rabbit every two or three weeks. In the beginning of the New Year the " Maple Charity " comes to them. It is a ticket for clothes or shoes to the value of 7s. 6d., and represents a bequest left primarily for widows and old couples; only when the former had all received tickets did married people with large families stand a chance. Two shillings comes from some other fund known as the " Jones Charity."

Mrs. Latimer's sister, who is in service, sends them all, or nearly all, her cast-off clothing; and Dolly is now helping in the same way. Dolly is Mrs. Latimer's oldest girl, who has now gone into service with a lady in the village. She has only been out six months, and all her wage is needed for her own outfit, but her mother reaps the benefit of whatever she dispenses with; and as there are children of all ages, almost anything can be made over into something for a smaller person. Mrs. Latimer makes jackets, knickers, trousers, and, in fact, all the clothing of the younger children, mainly out of her sister's " cast offs." Then out of a worn-out pair of socks or stockings she can always manufacture a smaller pair as good as new, or nearly. As we passed out she surveyed her husband's old green overcoat, hanging on the door, with an eye that discerned in it " a suit for Richard "—aged eleven—in the future. She also showed us the woollen scarves she had knitted for the children. Mr. Latimer himself does all the cobbling and mending for the family. He does no extra work in the village, " there are so many after any job that wants doing."

Of course his income, such as it is, is regular, save in illness. They are not in any club ; she has not been able to afford it.

The eldest boy, Robert, has just left school, and is looking out for a situation. He earned a shilling two weeks ago by acting as beater ; and two days this week he has been sawing wood for an old couple in the village, who give him his breakfast and dinner, though they will not be able to pay him more than a few pence. He comes back to " high tea."

Mrs. Latimer has some poultry—six hens at present—and calculates that she has cleared £1 with them this year. Moreover, in the spring she earned 17s. by picking stones off the land

for a farmer, taking the baby with her. Half
of this money went to the coal club, the other
half bought two pairs of shoes. The weekly
wage is quite absorbed in food and rent, and she
lays nothing by either for shoes or clothing. If
nothing extra is being earned, however, and the
purchase of shoes for one of the children is
inevitable, the provision bill is reduced; or, as
she expresses it, " When it comes to the come
to, we have to go short to buy shoes. But we
can't lay by for them."

There is no overtime whatever for this man.
He " works on the estate."

For breakfast all the children have porridge,
with sugar, some separated milk, and " a lump
of bread." They and the father take some food
—bread and margarine almost invariably—with
them, and tea and supper and dinner are merged
into one family meal at about 5.30, or later in
the summer.

There is a deficiency of 24 per cent. of protein
in this family's dietary, and of 7 per cent. of
energy value. Three per cent. of the food consumed is home produce.

EXPENDITURE DURING TYPICAL WEEK IN DECEMBER 1912.

	s.	d.		s.	d.
7 lbs. flour	1	0	7 pints separated milk .	0	3½
48 lbs. bread	6	0	2½ lbs. oatmeal . . .	0	5
4 lbs. sugar	0	8	Rent	2	0
½ lb. margarine (best) .	0	6	Tobacco	0	3½
½ lb. lard	0	4	Soap and soda . . .	0	2
½ lb. currants	0	2	Insurance	0	3
1 lb. pudding beef . .	0	7	Baking powder . . .	0	1
½ lb. suet	0	3½	Newspaper	0	1
½ lb. bacon	0	4	1 stone potatoes . . .	0	7
½ gallon oil	0	4½			
¼ lb. cocoa	0	4½		15	2
¼ lb. tea	0	4½			

HOME PRODUCE CONSUMED DURING THE WEEK.

9 lbs. parsnips. | 5 lbs. cabbage.

MENU OF MEALS PROVIDED DURING THE WEEK.

	BREAKFAST.	DINNER.	TEA.
SUN. . . .	Tea, bacon (for man), bread and dripping, porridge.	Meat pudding, parsnips, potatoes, currant dumpling.	Tea, bread and margarine.
MON. . . .	Tea, bread and margarine, porridge.	Bread and margarine or jam, tea.	Tea, remainder of vegetables and pudding from Sunday.
TUES. . . .	Tea, bread and margarine, porridge.	Bread and margarine or jam, tea.	Tea, suet pudding, greens, potatoes, bacon (for man).
WED. . . .	Tea, bread and margarine, porridge.	Bread and margarine or jam, tea.	Tea, suet pudding, jam, potatoes (for man only).
THUR. . .	Tea, bread and margarine or jam.	Bread and margarine or jam, tea.	Suet pudding, potatoes, bacon for man, dripping for children.
FRI. . . .	Tea, bread and margarine or jam, porridge.	Bread and jam or lard, tea.	Suet pudding, jam, parsnips, potatoes.
SAT. . . .	Tea, bread and jam, porridge.	Bread and margarine, tea.	Tea, scrap of bacon and bread for man, porridge for children.

Only the children have porridge for breakfast.

The man and the children take dinner with them. The man has a scrap of meat, bread and margarine or lard or jam, and cocoa. The children take bread and margarine or bread and lard. There is no supper.

4

Study No. XI.—North Riding of Yorkshire.

Man, wife, two sons aged five and one, and one daughter aged four.

TOTAL WEEKLY EARNINGS OF FAMILY.

Man's wage . . . . 15s.
(For a full week, which is exceptional.)

Extra earnings in the course of the year, £1, 16s.
Rent of cottage and garden, £8 per year.
Rent of common share land, 2s. 6d. per year.

The Knights are probably as hard up as any one in the village. If the man had regular work all the year round, he would only get 15s. a week for nine months and 18s. for three months in the year ; but in the winter his work is very irregular, and his average earnings are considerably less. If his father, himself only a working man with 17s. a week, liable to be docked by bad weather, did not give them a meal sometimes when nothing is coming in, they would have been more than half-starved many a time. It is a most demoralizing way of living for two people whose natural tendencies are all towards independence and respectability. Knight is a steady, capable-looking fellow. It is said of him by his neighbours that he can turn his hand to anything. But the farmer who was employing him regularly left the village some time ago, and since his departure the income has been precarious in the extreme. In the summer he can be pretty sure of work, but in the winter— !

" Last week he brought home 15s.," said Mrs. Knight, " but the week before it was only 4s. 6d."

When working irregularly, even in the winter, he gets paid at the rate of 3s. a day. And at present they are hoping for some thrashing, which would mean 3s. 6d. a day for a short time. Whether he will get it, however, seems quite uncertain.

Mrs. Knight is too fully occupied with the children to earn anything. She is still nursing the baby, and the elder ones are only five and nearly four years old respectively. In spite of hard living she is plump and rosy, a marked contrast to her husband, who is very thin and pale, though he looks fairly healthy.

They greatly value the produce of the garden, which is, roughly, says Mrs. Knight, " 18 yards by 80, counting the hedges and all." This year they sold some gooseberries out of it, and also a few potatoes, making altogether nearly £2. This

went towards the rent, which is very heavy—
£8 yearly. The house is sanitary and comparatively modern, and there is a pigsty. This
year they sold a pig for £3, 8s. They had had
it five months, and calculated that for the first
three months it cost them 1s. and for the last
two months 2s. a week in meal. It also consumed quantities of bad potatoes. They have a
few poultry, and promised to keep an account
of exactly what they make by them; but at
present it is next to nothing.

Knight, like the other villagers, has a " common
share " of land, for which he pays half a crown a
year. It is laid out to grass—this is the case
with most of them—and the use he makes of it
is to shoot a rabbit occasionally. Of course, this
means a gun licence—10s. a year—but it is worth
while. Sometimes one gets three rabbits, one
after another; though sometimes, on the other
hand, all the rabbits have made off into a neighbour's land, or have taken the scare altogether.
Still, at the rate of one every fortnight, they
more than pay for the licence. A rabbit lasts
two or three dinners; while if more than one
should be taken, the others are sold.

When we called it was one of Knight's un-employed days, but he was working hard in his garden. They have had some plums this year, which Mrs. Knight made into jam, and is now using. She made six stones, using three stones of sugar to three of plums.

They get potatoes all the year round as a rule, but as the last season was so very bad they may have to buy this year.

Like so many of these villagers, Mrs. Knight bakes half her flour into pastry and half into bread. This substantial, heavy pastry, in which a little home-made jam or a thin layer of cur-rants is, as it were, embedded like a streak of precious metal in sandstone, saves the butter, and is regarded as more satisfying than bread. She makes enough to last the week.

This week she herself earned a pound of liver, which appears in the budget, for help given to a butcher.

Here, as in the other Yorkshire budgets, some of the prices are rather high. Candles, for ex-ample, are two a penny. But dripping is bought cheap from a local institute.

No charities of any consequence are given in

the parish ; but Knight's own relatives, though badly off themselves, help to some extent with clothes, and occasionally there is a cast-off coat from some one for whom he has worked. Once a year a ladies' guild, run by a local celebrity, distributes garments to poor families, and this year Mrs. Knight got an apron.

We discussed the bill of fare for the current week. When Knight earns less, no meat and no lard or bacon are bought, and to some extent they become dependent on the help of his parents.

There is a deficiency of 34 per cent. of protein in this family's dietary, and of 11 per cent. of energy value. One-sixth of the food consumed is home produce, and 6 per cent. is payment for work.

EXPENDITURE DURING TYPICAL WEEK IN DECEMBER 1912.

	s.	d.		s.	d.
1¼ stones flour	2	2½	1½ cwt. coal	2	0
Yeast	0	1	Soap and washing pow-		
Baking powder	0	2½	ders	0	4
4⅔ pints new milk	0	7	½ gallon oil	0	5
½ lb. butter	0	8	Candles and matches	0	1
4 lbs. sugar	0	10	1 oz. tobacco	0	3½
¼ lb. tea	0	5	Insurance	0	3
1 lb. 14 oz. pie meat	0	11	Blacking, blacklead, laces	0	1½
2 lbs. dripping	0	6			
½ lb. bacon	0	5		11	2
1 lb. lard	0	8			
½ lb. currants	0	2			

The debts from previous week claimed the balance, and more, and nothing was laid aside towards the rent (3s. 1d. a week).

BUDGETS.

Home Produce consumed during the Week.

18 lbs. potatoes. 2 lbs. cabbage.

Rabbit.

Earned by the Woman.

1 lb. liver.

Menu of Meals provided during the Week.

	Breakfast.	Dinner.	Tea.
Sun. . .	Tea, bread and butter.	Meat pie, potatoes, cabbage, tea.	Tea, bread and butter or dripping, pastry.
Mon. . .	Tea, bread and butter or dripping.	Remains of Sunday's dinner, bread and butter, pastry, tea.	Tea, bread and butter, pastry.
Tues. . .	Tea, bread and butter or dripping.	Currant pudding, bread fried with dripping, tea.	Tea, bread and butter or dripping or jam, pastry.
Wed. . .	Tea, bread and butter or dripping.	Rabbit, potatoes, a little bacon, tea.	Tea, bread and butter or dripping.
Thur. .	Tea, bread and butter or dripping.	Remainder of rabbit, liver, bread, tea.	Tea, bread and butter or dripping, pastry.
Fri. . .	Tea, bread and scrape.	Bacon (for man), potatoes with dripping, pastry.	Tea, bread and scrape.
Sat. . .	Tea, bread and scrape.	Scrap of bacon (for man), bread and butter or dripping, pastry, tea.	Tea, bread and butter or dripping, pastry.

This family takes no supper.

Study No. XII.—Essex.

Man, wife, three sons aged ten, eight, and four, and two daughters aged thirteen and two.

TOTAL WEEKLY EARNINGS OF FAMILY.

Man's wage . . . . 15s.

Extra earnings in the course of the year, £6, 5s.
Rent of cottage and garden, 2s. per week.

The Borrows are a trifle better off in some respects than most of the other labourers of the district, since during the year Mr. Borrow earns a good deal of extra money. The farmer who employs him gives about £6, 10s. per man for the four weeks of harvest, 25s. being in lieu of beer money, an arrangement which suits Borrow well, as he has been a teetotaler for twenty-five years.

But that is not all. There is a sandpit on the land belonging to the farm, and lately, owing to the increase of building operations in the neighbourhood, sand has been in considerable demand, and there has been a good deal of " sand getting." This is piecework, and often means an additional 3s. weekly. Perhaps £4 extra in the year is earned by it, though Borrow found it difficult to calculate the exact amount.

There are no perquisites, except that this farmer, like various others in the district, allows his men to have potatoes by the bushel at wholesale prices. At Christmas, however, he gave Borrow 5s. and 4 lbs. of beef.

The village is not rich in charities; but Borrow remembers with real gratitude that when he was ill some months ago his mates clubbed together to give him 10s. He was not actually starving, since there was a little insurance money coming in, but the back rent was accumulating week by week.

Very occasionally a little extra money is earned by labourers in this district at other farms, when their own day's work is over. This happens chiefly at the thrashing season. Again, now and then, Borrow has done a bit of digging or cesspool emptying; but he has kept no record of the sums thus earned, and it is unlikely that they will amount to more than £1 or 25s. in the year. On the other hand, we must not forget that time is lost through bad weather. There is a saying in the neighbourhood that money lost by bad weather counterbalances the harvest money ; but probably a quick harvest will leave the men a little to the good.

There is a deficiency of 40 per cent. of protein in this family's dietary, and of 22 per cent. of energy value. All the food consumed is purchased.

EXPENDITURE DURING TYPICAL WEEK IN DECEMBER 1912.

	s.	d.		s.	d.
30 lbs. bread	3	9	3 lbs. savoys	0	3
½ stone flour	1	0	½ lb. suet	0	4
Baking powder and salt.	0	2	3 lbs. pork pieces . .	1	6
¾ lb. margarine . . .	0	6	Soap	0	3
¾ lb. lard	0	4½	Oil	0	3½
1½ lbs. marmalade . .	0	5½	½ cwt. coal	0	9
3 pints new milk . .	0	3½	Laces, thread, etc. . .	0	2
4 oz. cocoa . . .	0	4½	Newspapers	0	1½
4 oz. tea	0	4½	Rent	2	0
5 lbs. sugar	0	9½	Insurance	0	4
1 lb. jam	0	3			
½ lb. cheese	0	4½		15	2½
2 stones potatoes (whole-sale price)	0	6			

	BREAKFAST.	DINNER.	TEA.
SUN. . . .	Tea, bread and margarine.	Suet pudding, p o t a t o e s, greens, pork.	Tea, bread and margarine.
MON. . . .	Tea, bread and margarine.	Bread and margarine.	Suet pudding, potatoes.
TUES . . .	Tea, bread and lard.	Bread and marmalade.	Suet pudding, potatoes.
WED. . . .	Tea, bread and lard.	Bread and margarine.	Suet pudding, potatoes, turnips.
THUR.. . .	Tea, bread and margarine.	Bread and cheese.	Lard pudding, potatoes.
FRI. . . .	Tea, bread and lard.	Bread and cheese.	Potatoes, bread and lard.
SAT. . . .	Tea, bread and sugar.	Bread and jam.	P o t a t o e s, greens.

No supper is taken in this household.

Study No. XIII.—Essex.

Man, wife, three sons aged fifteen, thirteen, and eight, and three daughters aged ten, six, and two.

TOTAL WEEKLY EARNINGS OF FAMILY.

Wages—		*s.*	*d.*
Man		10	0
Son		5	0
Son		1	0
		16	0

Extra earnings in the course of the year, 24s. (18s. by the man and 6s. by the woman).

Rent of cottage and garden, 2s. per week.

The outlook of the Goodwin family on life is rather hopeless, though Goodwin is a steady, respectable workman, who has been under one master for some years. But his wife, though well meaning, is not " contriving." She is no hand at making the pastry which the labourer relies upon as more supporting than bread ; and if a rabbit is given to the household, she will only make it last one day. Such careless extravagance vexes the souls of her prudent neighbours, who, nevertheless, generally conclude their account of her failings by saying, " If she contrived and considered and did the utmost with every halfpenny, it isn't enough."

Just now, owing to an accident, Goodwin is on the club—it is to Mrs. Goodwin's credit that she has kept the club subscription going. He has 10s. a week coming in, which is, roughly speaking, equivalent to his average wage through the winter, since he has a great deal of off-time. It is said that the farmer for whom he works is responsible for the introduction of off-time into this village. Previously all the farmers had found some work for their regular men, even in bad weather; but Goodwin's wages have been known, in the worst weeks, to fall to 5s.

In the summer he averages about 14s. a week regularly—the wage is 2s. 4d. for a full day. At haymaking this spring he earned about 10s. extra; but the harvest only amounted to an additional shilling per week for eight weeks, owing to the weather. To some extent the winter's arrears are wiped off in the summer; but they would do very badly if the eldest boy was not bringing in 5s. a week. The second boy sometimes earns a few pence or scraps of food by running errands, or cleaning the knives for a lady. His mother kept no account of his earnings, which we have estimated quite roughly at what may be considered their outside limit, 1s. a week. A rabbit and three bloaters, entered as gifts, will cover his employer's help in kind.

Two elder girls are out in service, and help their mother to some extent with cast-off clothing, or a shilling or two in an emergency, but they cannot do a great deal.

The garden furnishes potatoes from the end of July to the end of December, and other vegetables or greens, used twice a week, for the greater part of the year. They have not yet finished their supply of greens, and will have more in the spring.

These people, like other poor families belonging to this parish, get the " Maple Charity "— 7s. 6d. worth of clothing—early in January. Again, Mrs. Goodwin earned 6s. this year by " three days tatering." In spite of these various additions to the man's wage, however, she is locally reported to be chronically in debt ; and doubtless her debts would be still heavier if tradespeople would supply her. The item " condensed milk," on which fivepence is spent, is an instance of her extravagance. A more strenuous woman would have contrived, even if she had to send the children a mile, to get separated milk, and spend threepence instead of fivepence, instead of saying feebly with Mrs. Goodwin that the separated couldn't be got.

Nevertheless, she is a kindly if an inefficient woman, and her husband is capable and intelligent enough. He will soon be back at work again, for his accident is not very serious, and though to be on the sick club really pays him almost as well as working, he prefers the latter method of making a living.

There is a deficiency of 24 per cent. of protein in this family's dietary, and of 17 per cent. of energy value. One-tenth of the food consumed is home produce, and one-thirteenth is given, though to some extent it may be regarded as a perquisite earned by the younger boy.

EXPENDITURE DURING TYPICAL WEEK IN DECEMBER 1912.

	s.	d.		s.	d.
56 lbs. bread	7	0	1 cwt. coal	1	4
¼ stone flour	0	6	Rent	2	0
4 lbs. sugar	0	10	Soap and soda . . .	0	3
1 lb. margarine . . .	0	8	6 oz. condensed milk .	0	5
½ lb. cheese	0	4½	4 bloaters	0	3
½ lb. tea	0	9	Oil and candles . . .	0	4
1¼ lbs. bacon	0	9	Insurance	0	3
1½ lbs. stewing steak and					
¼ lb. suet	1	0		16	8½

The income is outrun this week, though there is no entry for club contribution.

HOME PRODUCE CONSUMED DURING THE WEEK.

28 lbs. potatoes. | 18 lbs. greens.

GIFTS CONSUMED DURING THE WEEK.

3 bloaters. | 1 rabbit.

MENU OF MEALS PROVIDED DURING THE WEEK.

	BREAKFAST.	DINNER.	TEA.
SUN. . . .	Tea, bloaters, bread and margarine.	Suet pudding with meat, potatoes.	Bread and margarine, tea.
MON. . . .	Tea, toast with margarine.	Bread and margarine.	Greens, potatoes, bacon (for man and boy), bread, tea.
TUES. . . .	Tea, toast and margarine.	Tea, bread and margarine.	Rabbit stewed, potatoes, dumplings, tea.
WED. . . .	Tea, bread and margarine.	Tea, bread and margarine.	Greens, potatoes, bacon (for man and boy), tea.
THUR. . . .	Tea, bread and margarine.	Tea, bread and margarine.	Bloaters, bread and tea.
FRI. . . .	Tea, toast and margarine.	Tea, bread and scrape.	Bacon (for man and boy), potatoes, greens, tea.
SAT. . . .	Tea, bread and scrape.	Tea, bread and scrape.	Remainder of bacon, potatoes, tea.

The man and eldest boy take bread, cheese, and cold tea with them for dinner the first four days of the week; the last two days they take bread and margarine or bread and scrape and cold tea. The children attending school take bread and margarine with them for dinner.

This family takes no supper.

Study No. XIV.—Oxfordshire.

Man, wife, two sons aged eleven and a half and six, and one daughter aged eight and a half.

TOTAL WEEKLY EARNINGS OF FAMILY.

	s.	d.
Man's wage	14	0
Perquisites—		
Cottage and garden, say . . .	2	0
	16	0

Extra earnings in the course of the year, £3.

Mrs. Mayne is a slender little woman of forty, looking rather frail. She has had nine children, of whom only four are living. The eldest of these, a girl, is out in service, earning £9 a year. She has not been away long, and clothing expenses have been heavy, but she has contrived to help her mother with a pair of shoes for Ernie, the boy of six.

This woman is an excellent manager. She will sometimes go a mile and a half and back, with her neighbour, to gather wood to eke out the coal. She also gathers crab-apples, which she boils, together with vegetable marrows from the garden, to make jam for the children.

" There's hardly a week in the year when we're without jam," she says proudly. It is by virtue of the jam that the weekly bill for margarine, lard, or butter is reduced to a shilling. In the summer, when less coal is needed, butter is mainly used, but as coal and oil absorb more of the weekly income, margarine—popularly known as " overweight butter "—takes the place of butter proper. Sometimes lard is used on the bread instead of either.

" Do you often get bones for soup ? " asked the investigator, who was tired of being reproached with the apathy of the poor with regard to soup and bones. No, Mrs. Mayne didn't. The butcher she dealt with, at the " chilled meat " shop, hardly ever had any bones to dispose of, and was not given to selling them cheaply when he had. Such facilities for inexpensive meals are largely a matter of favour. And the Maynes were plutocrats compared to many people —not a family for whom a kindly dealer would set aside cheap bones.

Mr. Mayne earns 14s. a week and his cottage, a four-roomed cottage with a pantry, a good-sized garden, and a potato patch, 20 poles, free.

There is a little overtime at haymaking, but no more than is absorbed by extra food for the breadwinner. At Michaelmas, however, there is a solid £2, and generally another £1 is made by thatching. These extra sums of money are spent chiefly in clothing. Last year, however, half the Michaelmas money went for a doctor's bill.

Mrs. Mayne has a sister in another part of the country, a trifle better off than herself, who sends her all the old clothing she can, and she " makes all the clothes herself," cutting down and cutting up in fine style. But when all her skill has been brought into play, there are still shoes to consider, and clothes for the man, socks and stockings, and any incidental expense incurred, or any bill that has been allowed to run. Sometimes an article of clothing is bought on the instalment system of an " outrider " from some market town within range ; but this is really a comparatively expensive method of purchase.

Last year Mr. Mayne earned himself a whole pair of shoes, at 7s. 11d., by mole-catching. He gets a penny each for the moles caught, and then skins them and sells the furs for a penny each.

But this year he has been less lucky, and his shoes had to come out of the Michaelmas money. He is really an abstemious man, but he likes " a quart of ale and a glass of beer on a Saturday," costing 5½d.*   He also gets through, when he can afford it, two ounces of tobacco.   But these luxuries, in the depth of winter, sometimes have to be curtailed.

" And that is all he earns ?   Is there nothing extra for hoeing ? "

" No ; when he does any hoeing, it comes in the day's work.   But very occasionally, if there's some errand at a distance, or some job that's out of his beat, he'll get sixpence from the master. And if he happens to be out shooting with him, he'll get a rabbit.   And he let him have some windfalls from the apple trees this autumn, pretty near two stones.   Oh, he's not bad to us. Last year, when my husband was ill six weeks, he bought us a joint of mutton, fresh from the butcher's—brought it to the house himself ! "

" You don't keep a pig, do you ? "

" Oh no, we're not allowed to keep pigs—not

---

* The cheapest beer, sold at 1½d. a pint, goes under the name of "ale."   By " beer " the countryman usually means a better quality, sold at 2d. or 2½d. a pint.

so much as rabbits. But we're a lot better off than some."

The Maynes, on the whole, have been on good terms with their employers, for one of whom Mayne worked twelve years for 13s. and his house, in an outlying village. Then came three months with an obviously impossible person, who " locked up everything." The old employer had trusted his head men; the other " reckoned to go away for Christmas, and had to come back on Christmas-day morning to give out the stores for the cattle "—a proceeding bitterly resented.

" Naturally your husband has to work on Sundays, being a cowman ? "

" Oh yes. The cottage counts for Sunday work. There are the cows to milk and the pigs to feed; but just now he only has to go twice on Sunday—about three hours' work altogether. And now the days are short (November) he gets his breakfast at 6.30, and begins work at 7. He takes some bread and cheese with him, if there's any cheese left; and if there isn't, he waits till dinner-time. There was no cheese left this morning ! "

Mrs. Mayne cooks a hot dinner of some kind every day, though towards the end of the week meat runs short. Sometimes only a 1s. is spent on chilled meat, and later on in the week they buy a good-sized rabbit for 10d. (selling the skin for a 1d.). This lasts them two dinners, and even provides the man with a taste for breakfast.

Mayne himself is a great contrast to his wife —a tall, broad-shouldered man of " five foot ten and a half inches," who, when they first came to this house, was always " banging his head against the beam " when he passed through the door. As it is, inside the room, his head almost touches the ceiling—there is certainly not more than a quarter of an inch grace ! They are a good type, active to their finger-ends, capable, " contriving," missing no opportunity of turning an honest penny—withal, sincere, cheery, and kindly. But when all is said and done, life is a continual struggle. To be sure, the garden, as Mrs. Mayne says, is " half the battle." But the garden can only be made to provide them with vegetables for the year by hard toil, given by a man who is already toiling hard through a long working day, and never knows what it is even to have a Sunday free. Still the Maynes do not grumble.

In the budget not a penny is allowed even for cotton. This, with the clothing, comes out of any extra money earned. If no clothing were given, they would have to cut down the food bill.

There is a deficiency of 21 per cent. of protein in this family's dietary. One-twelfth of the food consumed is home produce.

EXPENDITURE DURING TYPICAL WEEK IN NOVEMBER 1912.

	s.	d.		s.	d.
36 lbs. bread	4	1½	Soap, soda, blue, matches,		
¼ stone flour	0	5½	etc.	0	3½
7 lbs. sugar	1	2	1 quart oil and candles .	0	3½
1 lb. cheese	0	9	¼ lb. tea	0	4½
1 quart new milk.	0	3	1 pint beer and 1 quart		
2 lbs. margarine .	1	0	ale	0	5½
5 lbs. chilled beef	1	10½	Baking powder	0	1
¼ lb. suet	0	1½	Insurance	0	4
1¼ lbs. currant cake .	0	4½			
1 cwt. coal	1	4		14	0
2 oz. tobacco .	0	7			
Salt, blacking, etc.	0	1½			

HOME PRODUCE CONSUMED DURING THE WEEK.

18 lbs. potatoes.	1 lb. turnips.
2½ lbs. carrots.	1 lb. onions.

4 lbs. greens.

GIFTS CONSUMED DURING THE WEEK.

2½ lbs. apples.

MENU OF MEALS PROVIDED DURING THE WEEK.

	BREAKFAST.	DINNER.	TEA.	SUPPER.
SUN.	Tea, meat for man, bread and butter.	Meat pudding, potatoes, carrots.	Tea, bread and butter or jam, cake.	Tea, bread and butter or cheese.
MON.	Tea, bread and butter or jam, little meat (for man).	Meat pudding warmed up, potatoes.	Tea, bread and butter or jam.	Tea, bread and butter or cheese.
TUES.	Tea, bread and lard or jam.	Stewed meat, potatoes, sprouts, onions.	Tea, bread and butter or lard or jam, meat for man.	Bread and butter or cheese.
WED.	Tea, bread and butter or jam, little meat (for man).	Roast meat, baked potatoes, greens.	Tea, bread and butter or jam.	Bread and cheese or butter.
THUR.	Tea, bread and butter or lard or jam.	Irish stew, onions, carrots, turnips, potatoes.	Tea, bread and jam or lard or butter.	Bread and jam.
FRI.	Tea, bread and jam or butter, scrap of meat (for man).	Apple pudding.	Tea, bread and jam or butter.	None.
SAT.	Tea, bread and jam.	Potatoes, dumplings.	Tea, bread and jam.	Tea, bread and butter.

Only the man and wife have a little supper.

The man takes a little bread and cheese with him to eat between breakfast and dinner about two or three days each week.

Study No. XV.—North Riding of Yorkshire.

Man, wife, two sons aged six and three, and one daughter aged ten.

TOTAL WEEKLY EARNINGS OF FAMILY.

Man's wage . . . . 16s.

The extra earnings in the course of the year are uncertain. Rent of cottage and garden, £5, 5s. per year, rates 15s. per year.

The Bartons would, they say, find it almost impossible to live if the children who are out in service did not help those at home. What they give from time to time practically covers the rent, which is £5, 5s. yearly. There are also rates, to the amount of 15s. yearly; but Barton tries to lay something by towards them in the summer.

He is a " road-scraper " for more than eight months in the year, and a labourer on the land for more than three. From the end of harvest to the beginning of hay-time he earns 16s. a week, but not quite regularly. This winter, for instance, he calculates that he has lost at least 10s. through bad weather. In the haytime, however, he generally earns 18s. a week, for three weeks. For the next few weeks, till the harvest, the average is a little less, as not being the regular man of any one farmer, he nearly always loses some odd days. But later on, if the harvest is good, he is pretty certain to earn 25s. weekly for four weeks. Last year, unfortunately, the weather was so bad that there was hardly any extra money to be earned.

It is this varying summer money that must meet the clothing expenses of five people—there are three children at home, aged ten, six, and three. It cannot be expected that the children who are away will do more than help with the rent, and possibly the rates. They have their own personal expenses. Two sons are in farm service, one girl is living with a farmer's family, and the other, though in service, is very delicate, and cannot help at all, having to spend a great part of her small wage on medicine and doctors' bills.

In this respect, the Bartons themselves are hampered. Four years ago, a doctor's bill of ten guineas was incurred, which they are still gradually paying off—another claim on the

" summer money." It was for Mrs. Barton, who had a very serious operation. Though she keeps the house neat and clean, and does an endless amount of making and mending, she is very far from strong. Her husband, too, might be stronger, though he has never been off work through illness since he had an accident three years ago, and was laid aside for some weeks. As for Nora, the eldest child at home, she is a thin slip of a girl, too tall for her age, and very pale. The whole family, directly or indirectly, is suffering from chronic anxiety, over-work, and under-feeding. They are intensely respectable people, to whom the precarious nature of their income and its inadequacy are peculiarly distressing.

Knowing that the elder children were living at some distance, we said, " Isn't there anything to be allowed for stamps ? "

" No," said Mrs. Barton; and then, with a depth of suppressed worry in her voice, " I get into worse trouble for not writing than any woman in England ; we can't afford stamps ! "

There is little in the village to distract their minds from their own troubles. Asked if religion, in the form of attendance at some place of worship, was any help, Mr. Barton grinned broadly, and Mrs. Barton said dubiously,—

" Oh yes, it helps—a bit."

The officiating minister, however, was very " doly." And life was already " doly " enough.

There is a deficiency of 14 per cent. of protein in this family's dietary, and of 7 per cent. of energy value. All the food is purchased.

EXPENDITURE DURING TYPICAL WEEK IN FEBRUARY 1913.

	s.	d.		s.	d.
2 stones flour . . .	3	4	½ lb. liver, ¼ lb. suet, and		
Yeast and baking powder	0	4½	5 lbs. beef	2	10½
1 lb. lard	0	7	1 stone potatoes . . .	0	6
1 lb. margarine . . .	0	6	1 oz. tobacco	0	3½
11 eggs	1	0	1 cwt. coal	1	3
3 pints new milk and 1			1 lb. soap	0	3
quart separated . .	0	5½	Oil, candles, and matches	0	4
6 oz. tea	0	6	Insurance, newspaper .	0	5
¼ lb. cocoa	0	4½			
2 lbs. sugar	0	4½		15	2
½ lb. currants . . .	0	2	Balance towards clothes,		
1 lb. golden syrup . .	0	3	rates, and debt . .	0	10
½ lb. curds and 1 lb. jam	0	8			
½ lb. rice	0	1		16	0
1 lb. pie pieces . . .	0	7			

HOME PRODUCE CONSUMED DURING THE WEEK.
3 oz. onions.

Menu of Meals provided during the Week.

	BREAKFAST.	DINNER.	TEA.
SUN. . . .	Tea, bread and margarine, egg (for man), 2 eggs shared between others.	Roast beef, Yorkshire pudding, potatoes, cocoa.	Tea, bread and margarine or golden syrup, cake, pastry.
MON. . . .	Tea, bread and margarine or golden syrup, meat (for man).	Cold beef, bread and margarine, pastry, cocoa.	Tea, bread and margarine or golden syrup, cake, pastry.
TUES. . . .	Tea, cocoa, bread and margarine, egg (for man), egg shared by woman with children.	Fried beef, potatoes, suet dumplings with currants, cocoa.	Tea, bread and margarine, pastry.
WED. . . .	Tea, cocoa, bread and margarine, meat (for man).	Hash, potatoes, dumplings with gravy or syrup, cocoa.	Tea, bread and margarine or golden syrup, pastry.
THUR. . . .	Tea, cocoa, bread and margarine or golden syrup, egg (for man).	Fried liver, potatoes, Yorkshire pudding, tea.	Tea, bread and margarine or golden syrup, pastry.
FRI. . . .	Tea, bread and margarine, egg (for man), egg shared between others.	Meat pie, rice pudding, tea or cocoa.	Tea, bread and margarine or golden syrup, pastry.
SAT. . . .	Tea, bread and margarine or golden syrup, pastry.	Remainder of meat pie, bread and margarine, tea or cocoa.	Tea, bread and margarine or golden syrup, pastry.

This family takes no supper.

Study No. XVI.—Berkshire.

Man, wife, five daughters aged twelve, ten, nine, six, and two.

TOTAL WEEKLY EARNINGS OF FAMILY.

	s.	d.
Man's wage	14	0
Perquisites—		
Cottage and garden, say	2	0
	16	0

Extra earnings in the course of the year, £2, 5s.
Rent of allotment, 5s. per year.

Mr. and Mrs. Harry Finch are a typical couple —hard-working and honest, who neither ask for nor receive help from people who are better off, though sometimes old Mrs. Finch, who has two sons working, passes on a well-worn black dress to Mrs. Harry.

The village is a poor one, in which charities are almost unknown, even at Christmas.

" Some of those that go to chapel get a hundred of coal, I believe," says Mrs. Finch. " But the vicar don't give anything away. Farmer Bell used to give a piece of beef to some of his men ; but it led to words among

them, and so he said he would give it up altogether."

It must be noted that the income practically
has to cover clothing for the family. Old Mrs.
Finch's cast-off dresses cannot amount to much.
She herself is poor. We first saw her daughter-
in-law at her house, and the midday meal was
set for the family—on a Wednesday, when the
week's supplies are not supposed to be exhausted.
It consisted of potatoes, turnips, and bread, and
a fearsome-looking dish known as " pigs' teeth,"
which seemed to be the bony palate of a pig,
with no flesh on it. But old Mrs. Finch explained
that it " looked better than nothing." One
hardly realizes to what extent the very poor, on
whose labour we are all dependent, have to live
on what is popularly described as " offal."

Harry Finch " goes with the engine," so that
he earns rather more than the ordinary labourer
in this village. We were a long while trying to
find out exactly how much he did earn. He has
a cottage free, and every week he retains 1s.
for pocket-money, out of which he pays for his
insurance, and treats himself to a certain amount
of beer. Never, even in the summer, does he

bring home more than 13s. For the last three weeks he has averaged 12s.—13s. one week, 11s. another, 12s. another—and it will soon drop to 11s. again. But through the summer he brings home 13s. pretty regularly. This, however, includes " extra time ; " there is no Michaelmas money. He himself is not quite clear as to how his income averages out.

" How much *do* you earn ? "

" I earns a smart lot more than I gets," says Harry Finch good-naturedly.

And there seems to be no doubt about that. We discussed the subject of vegetables. They have a garden, and also rent 20 poles at 5s. a year. This supplies them with potatoes at the rate of seven pounds a day for eight months in the year, and other vegetables or greens for six months, taking the outside estimate. Of course greens or turnips or parsnips are not used at the same rate. They cook a few every day, but only about a pound. That corresponds roughly to other families of six or seven people who may cook larger quantities, but less frequently. Twice a week, or perhaps three times, for greens, turnips, or parsnips is common. But nearly everywhere potatoes are the staple dish, and the quantity of other vegetables used is much less.

" Potatoes have more stay in them ! " said one villager, with deplorable ignorance of food values. When possible, a little margarine is eaten with the potatoes.

Mrs. Finch told us that this year she could not have pulled through and kept out of debt if she herself, with the help of the children—there are five girls, from two to twelve years of age— had not gleaned, or " leesed," three sacks of corn.

" Isn't leesing all done with ? "

" So it is everywhere else, but not here ! "

She had sold the corn at 15s. a sack, and the 45s. had wiped off the debts for clothing that are so difficult to meet out of the labourer's wage, when one is lucky if one can lay by sixpence a week.

She gave us a literal account of how she managed in a good week in the winter, a week in which she had 13s. clear. In the summer, of course, less fuel is needed ; but in her case —and in very many cases—the supply of vege- tables is exhausted by the end of March at the very latest ; and that means either an additional outlay on potatoes or on bread.

When she has less than 13s., she makes 1 cwt. of coal last the week, and the meat bill goes down from 1s. 6d. to 1s. The cheap lard, too, sometimes has to be forgone.

The meat is " chilled." Very occasionally, threepennyworth of herrings or bloaters is bought on a Friday. Currants are very seldom bought. The finances " don't run to " syrup or jam, though last year Mrs. Finch made a few pounds of gooseberry jam, taking the gooseberries out of the garden. It was soon consumed by the children.

The house was beautifully neat and clean, and so was the little girl who had stayed at home from school for a cold. But she looked delicate and anæmic.

The meat is eaten, here as elsewhere, almost entirely by the man. Mrs. Finch is called upon, by the way, to furnish his ounce of tobacco.

" What would you do if I was to take that pipe off of you ? " said one woman in this village to her husband.

" It's all I have ! " he replied.

There is a deficiency of 25 per cent. of protein in this family's dietary, and of 14 per cent. of energy value. One-sixth of the food consumed is home produce.

EXPENDITURE DURING TYPICAL WEEK IN NOVEMBER 1912.

	s.	d.		s.	d.
40 lbs. bread	4	7	Soap and soda . . .	0	2½
¼ stone flour	0	5½	1¼ cwt. coal	1	6
7 pints skim milk . .	0	3½	1 oz. tobacco	0	3½
½ lb. cheese	0	4½			
2 lbs. margarine . . .	1	0		12	8
4 lbs. sugar	0	8			
½ lb. tea	0	8	Man's pocket money, in-		
¼ lb. chocolate powder .	0	2	cluding insurance .	1	0
½ lb. lard	0	3½			
4¼ lbs. frozen meat and				13	8
¼ lb. mutton chop .	1	6	Balance put aside for		
½ lb. suet	0	2	shoes, etc.	0	4
1 quart oil	0	2½			
Wood (farthing bundles)	0	3½		14	0

HOME PRODUCE CONSUMED DURING THE WEEK.

49 lbs. potatoes.	1 lb. turnips.
4 lbs. sprouts.	1 lb. savoys.
1 lb. parsnips.	6 oz. onions.

Menu of Meals provided during the Week.

	BREAKFAST.	DINNER.	TEA.	SUPPER.
SUN. .	Bread and margarine, tea.	Roast beef, suet pudding, sprouts, potatoes.	Tea, bread and margarine.	Bread and cheese.
MON.	Bread and margarine, tea.	Cold meat, potatoes, sprouts.	Tea, bread and margarine.	Bread and cheese.
TUES.	Bread and margarine, tea.	Cold meat, potatoes, sprouts, tea.	Tea, bread and margarine.	Bread and cheese.
WED.	Bread and margarine, tea.	Stewed meat (with onion), potatoes, savoys, tea.	Tea, bread and margarine.	Bread and cheese.
THUR.	Bread and margarine, tea.	Meat (stewed again with onion), potatoes, turnips.	Tea, bread and lard.	Bread and lard, tea.
FRI. .	Bread and lard, tea.	Potatoes and sprouts, bread and margarine, tea.	Tea, bread and lard.	Bread and lard, cocoa.
SAT. .	Bread and margarine, tea.	Mutton chop (for man), potatoes, parsnip, tea.	Tea, bread and lard.	Bread and cheese, cocoa.

Study No. XVII.—Essex.

Man, wife, two sons, aged nine and four, and four daughters, aged eleven, seven, two, and three months.

TOTAL WEEKLY EARNINGS OF FAMILY.

	s.	d.
Man's wage	15	0
Perquisites—		
Cottage and garden, say	2	0
	17	0

Extra earnings in the course of the year, £1, 13s. 6d.

The Burts are thoroughly respectable, hard-working folk. They have 15s. a week and the cottage in which they live. The amount of over-time money earned by Burt throughout the past year has been £1, 13s. 6d., and the additional work for which it was paid involved additional outlay on food.

There are six children, ranging from eleven years old to three months. Up to last year Mrs. Burt herself earned a little ; but this year she has been suffering from a bad leg, so that even if she could leave the baby, it would be impossible for her to go out to work.

However it may be with the rich, misfortunes never come singly to the poor, and Mrs. Burt's father, who was employed at a gasworks in London, and often sent her a shilling, is ill this year and on his club.

The last substantial good turn he did her was to send her some ,fowls ; but some of them had to be sold to buy shoes and shirts for her husband ; and she has only three hens left, which at present are not laying. They are fed with a mixture of potato peelings and " middlings," the latter costing about 1½d. a week. It does not sound exactly the kind of diet which will inspire hens to lay very many eggs.

Burt's hours are from 5 a.m. to 5.30 p.m., with half an hour for breakfast and an hour for dinner. He is a horseman. On Sundays he goes twice to look after his charge, but is only at work about three hours. He gets no perquisites, and the village is not wealthy; they have few Christmas charities, though they will probably get a local charity of 7s. 6d. worth of clothing this year.

We had some difficulty in puzzling out the daily bill of fare, as it varied—within certain narrow limits—from week to week. For instance, the pound of currants, which is put down for this particular week, is sometimes replaced by jam. Mrs. Burt made 23 lbs. of blackberry jam this year, and has been using it at intervals, saving it for the weeks in which it was impossible to buy currants. She is afraid that when she does use it she uses a 3-lb. jar in a week; but in such weeks she only gets half a pound of margarine instead of a pound.

The coal bill is notably moderate. This is because the family has been " very lucky " with wood. A tree blew down on the farm not long ago, and Burt has been allowed to take a good deal of it for fuel. They have also managed to get coal cheaper by buying the half-ton and paying 1s. weekly. But in spite of all thrift and all efforts, they are in debt.

" Do you owe as much as £10 ? " we said.

" I should hope not! I was saying to my husband only the other day, if any one gave me £5, I would pay every penny I owed and have a nice shilling over to spend ! "

The local shopkeeper speaks well of Mrs. Burt's honesty.

A sewing-machine on the table is in pretty constant use, though the expenditure on clothes is at present a negligible item. Early last year Mrs. Burt helped to replenish the family wardrobe by mangold-weeding; but, as already explained, she cannot work this year.

There is a garden, but it has only supplied them with potatoes from the beginning of August to the end of the first week in December. At present—December 12—they have to buy them.

The little children who go to school take their dinners with them, chiefly bread and butter, with a taste of cake or pastry if possible. The father comes home to dinner, and if any vegetables or puddings are cooked, the children's shares are reserved.

The meat bill given for this week is very typical. They can only spend more than 1s. on meat if any relative of the woman's gives or sends them 1s., which, as explained above, very seldom happens now.

" I often lie awake planning if I could do any different," said the wife.

She uses oatmeal for herself because of the

baby. But they very seldom buy rice. " They won't make a whole meal of it," she explains. " They think it's an extra, so it don't really come cheap ! "

No cheese, no bacon, no candles, but bed at 8 p.m. Even so, they are compelled to use a quart of oil in the winter. Asked if she insured herself or the children, Mrs. Burt said, " No ; I put it in their bellies when they're alive ; it's no use paying for them when they're dead. Somebody'll bury them ! And when they're dead they won't want nothing ! "

The husband's sisters help to some extent with cast-off clothing. Last year the children earned a trifle by picking up acorns, which they sold by the bushel to feed pigs. Florrie also earned the large amount of 4½d. for blackberries gathered.

" Ought we to put something down for needles and thread every week ? "

" Well, I generally contrive to get them out of my rags and bones."

We did not ask exactly what constituted a rag for which no further use could be found in Mrs. Burt's vocabulary. And the bones, with a butcher's bill of 1s. weekly, must have required some hoarding.

There is a deficiency of 27 per cent. of protein in this family's dietary, and of 9 per cent. of energy value. One per cent. of the food consumed is home produce.

EXPENDITURE DURING TYPICAL WEEK IN DECEMBER 1912.

	s.	d.		s.	d.
1 stone flour	2	0	Soap, soda, blacking, blacklead, matches, hearthstone, etc. . .	0	4
38 lbs. bread	4	6			
½ lb. dripping . . .	0	3			
1 lb. currants . . .	0	4	Coal	1	0
7 lbs. sugar	1	2	1½ oz. tobacco . . .	0	6
1 lb. margarine . . .	0	8	1 quart oil	0	2½
½ lb. lard	0	3½	Insurance	0	3
3 quarts separated milk.	0	3	Food for fowls . . .	0	1½
1¾ lbs. flank beef and ¼ lb. suet	1	0		14	7
7 oz. tea	0	7	Balance for shoes and clothes, etc. . . .	0	5
¼ lb. chocolate powder .	0	1			
1 stone potatoes . . .	0	7		15	0
2 lbs. fine oatmeal . .	0	4			
Baking powder . . .	0	1½			

HOME PRODUCE CONSUMED DURING THE WEEK.

3 lbs. parsnips. | 4 lbs. swedes.

	BREAKFAST.	DINNER.	TEA.	SUPPER.
SUN. .	Tea, bread and mar-garine, gruel.	Roast beef, suet dump-lings, pota-toes, pars-nips, cur-rant pud-ding.	Tea, bread and mar-garine, cake.	Porridge (for w o m a n only).
MON. .	Tea, bread and mar-garine, gruel.	Vegetables (left from S u n d a y), cold meat, c o c o a, b r e a d, pastry.	Tea, bread and mar-garine, cake.	Porridge (for w o m a n only).
TUES. .	Tea, bread, gruel.	Bread and margarine, tea.	Tea, bread and mar-garine.	Porridge (for w o m a n only).
WED. .	Tea, bread and mar-garine, gruel.	Dumplings, bread and lard, pota-toes, tea.	Tea, bread and drip-ping.	Porridge (for w o m a n only).
THUR.	Tea, bread and mar-garine, gruel.	Potatoes and swedes with drip-ping, tea.	Tea, bread and drip-ping.	Porridge (for w o m a n only).
FRI. .	Tea, bread and mar-garine, gruel.	Potatoes, c u r r a n t dumpling, bread and margarine, pastry.	Tea, bread and mar-garine, pastry.	Porridge (for w o m a n only).
SAT. .	Tea, bread and mar-garine, gruel.	Bread and margarine, tea.	Tea, bread and mar-garine.	Porridge (for w o m a n only).

The school children eat their share of dinner at teatime.

Study No. XVIII.—North Riding
of Yorkshire.

Man, wife, five daughters, aged eight, seven.
five, two, and one.

TOTAL WEEKLY EARNINGS OF FAMILY.

	s.	d.
Man's wage	9	0
Perquisites—		
Man's board, say	8	0
	17	0

Extra earnings in the course of the year, £1.
Rent of cottage and garden, 1s. 11d. per week.

The Arthurs live in what it would perhaps be
most correct to describe as a " two-roomed cottage with extras." There is a rough loft, used
in cases of emergency by all the children, and
always by the two elder children; there are a wash-
house, and a kind of pantry-scullery occupied by
the shoes of the family, an ancient bicycle, and
the frame used by Mrs. Arthur when she is
making hearthrugs. The provisions, too, are
kept there on the shelf.

But there are only two comfortable rooms—
the kitchen and bedroom on the ground floor.

Both are good-sized as cottage accommodation goes.

There is a bright fire in the living-room, but it is very obviously the abode of poverty. There is no carpet on the stone floor, but a good-sized hearthrug and a smaller rug, both of them made out of clippings by Mrs. Arthur, and two small bits of sacking. The place is clean and fresh. The wall would do with a new paper—the last, as Mrs. Arthur explains, having been put on when " there weren't so many of 'em." But it is not likely to get it. Four or five almanacs are hung up, and on the mantelpiece are two gaudy advertisements, duplicates of " Price's Child's Night Lights," two old vases, a clock, and various tins. There are five wooden chairs, including a small high-chair, a stool, and a wooden cradle.

As for the bedroom, it is pretty fully occupied by the two large bedsteads in which five Arthurs are dispersed at nights—father, mother, and baby in one bed; two children, aged five and three, in the other. There is no carpet on the red-brick floor. A chest of drawers faces the beds.

The Arthurs have been married nine years, during which time Arthur has been working regularly winter and summer for one farmer, for 9s. a week, paid fortnightly, and his food. The food comprises three square meals, with bacon for breakfast and tea, or supper, at 6 p.m., and beef, or perhaps mutton, for dinner, with apple pies, dumplings, " sad-cakes," or whatever it happens to be.

" Last year," he says, " t' farmer offered me 16s. a week and to meat misel, but 'taint sie good as the 9s. and 'im meatin' me."

Doubtless the family as a whole might profit better for a time by the 16s. a week ; but here, as elsewhere, the health of the breadwinner must be the first consideration. Arthur works hard for his wage, from 6 a.m. to 6 p.m., and also on Sundays. He has an hour off for dinner, but hardly a quarter of an hour for breakfast. In the summer he has to milk twice a day, and " fodder t' stock " at dinner-time. In the winter there is a sheepfold to look after, and Sunday is nearly as hard as any other day.

" It's bed and wark wi' Arthur, poor thing," said a sympathetic villager. " He's nobbut had three days holiday sen he were married. An', rightly speakin', that weren't holidays like ; yah tahm was when he went to t' show for his maister, and t'other tahm he was ill i' bed. To be sewer he went to Pedley (the nearest market town) las' Soondah. That war marvellous! He milked before he set out to walk, and he got anuther man to fodder an' milk at neet."

Arthur is well liked in the village. He is a steady, hard-working, pleasant-faced, stalwart fellow; but the hard life is telling on him, and he looks more weary than a man of thirty-one years should look. Sometimes, too, his voice has a despondent ring, even though the next moment he will laugh heartily at a droll speech from his wife or the children's pranks.

"The childer are fair crazed aboot their dad," says Mrs. Arthur. She is a small, fair, energetic, and somewhat combative woman, who works hard, even furiously, making, mending, washing, cleaning, and baking, but who is said by the neighbours to be "not much good at plannin'." Her bill of fare is more uncertain than that of most of the villagers. Sometimes she bakes more bread and uses fewer vegetables; sometimes, especially when the grocer's bill is getting too far in arrears, she tries to dispense

with bread and live on turnips and carrots or
potatoes out of the large garden at which Arthur
works in the long evenings.

The two quarrel sometimes, or, in a village
parlance, " turn dark tongues to each uther "—a
proceeding which is not considered edifying for
the children, who " learn that kind of talk soon
enough, without hearing it at home." But they
are sincerely attached to one another and to the
little ones, who look happy, clean, and fairly
healthy.

They regard church or chapel going as an expensive, even a prohibitive, luxury, which is apt
to have a deteriorating effect on those who indulge in it. Mrs. Arthur only the day before
had been asked by a neighbour why she never
attended any place of worship. " I said to her,
' No, I doant gan to chapel, no mair dis he, and
we bean't no worse'n them as dea. There's sum
on 'em as'll pray and talk good at chapel, an'
they'll sit doon to sike a meal as *we* could niver
set doon to, and then they'll 'unger t' stock.
There's Redington ; 'e's fair 'ungered three 'orses
to death, and when t' next dees 'e'll 'appen ask
some of they ministers to raht a letter for 'im

an' go collectin' for anuther. But Arthur, I'll say this for 'im, 'e'd sooner 'unger hissen than t' stock. No, we deant 'old with chapel going. 'Taint the cleas; I'd go as I am, if I *did* go. If fooaks wanted me any differ, they could take t' claes off their awn backs and gi' 'em to me to put on.' "

So Mrs. Arthur, in her most defiant spirit. But even the defiance has an undercurrent of strained anxiety. In spite of the regularity of the pay, such as it is, and the kindliness of neighbours, and the large garden, with its couple of fruit trees and ample supply of vegetables, the life is hard—almost impossible. Only the other day she broke out to a neighbour as poor as herself. " I's sewer money, it seems to awnt me day and neet. I cawn't reest for it; I doan't know t' reason on't. If it wasn't for t' wark I should go all wrang. I dean't like to be owing; I'd pay to t' last awpenny, look ye, and I dean't know 'ow to live any differ. I niver gies t' bairns a awpenny. I niver allows 'em to go for goodies—if I niver starts 'em they'll niver want. If they iver has a farden it's what other fooaks gi'es 'em, an' often I takes that frae 'em. I cawn't do no mair'n I can, and yet I disn't sleep for troublin'. Last neet I was out o' bed four times with t' lail 'un, an' then I sat ower on t' bed ruing. An' I had a good rue, and I felt a bit better.

" But I isn't a rogue, look yer, an' if I had t' money I wadn't get things wi'out payin'. I ain't bowt meat nor bacon for weeks an' weeks. I get a bit o' lard and meeak some sad-cakes for t' childer an' mysen. I feel as if I mun hae sumethin' I can eat, an' it saves t' butter. *He* niver bites at home—nobbut a drink o' tea—he'd think it would be takkin' it oot of our mooths. But t' kids is that 'ungry, I tell yer, they'd eat me up if I was meat an' bread an' stuff—they would, I'se sewer ! I told a man I owes two shillings would 'e take five kids instead. But he said he niver took 'em by less ner t' awf-dozen ! "

Mrs. Arthur's debts, when taken together, perhaps do not seem so appalling. There is £1, 1s. 6d. for shoes, at three different shops within a radius of six miles, about 5s. at one grocer's and about 4s. at another. There is the 2s. above mentioned, incurred for towels, bought in before the last confinement. And there are doctor's bills amounting to 26s. The rent book is clear. But these debts are mak-

ing an old woman of Mrs. Arthur, though she is
only twenty-six. She is overworked and underfed—and they are all the latter, even the baby.

"*That* little customer wants sarvin' three times
a day wi' bried an' milk an' sugar; an' she
could eat more—they all could."

The harvest money is only £1, and that is the
one extra allowed. This year part of it was
mortgaged to the farmer for insurance and the
weekly half-pound of butter. The rest wiped off
some arrears, but not the whole. Twelve shillings went for rent. Arthur's master is not
liberal with gifts, although last year he did give
him " a glazy coat " (mackintosh) for shepherding.

They have only other people's " cast-offs " to
rely upon in the matter of clothing.

" If we didn't hae cleas given, we suld hae to
black oorsels ower an' go naykt," says Mrs. Arthur.

Last week her mother had given her a pound
of curds, and this week her brother—both living
in a town ten miles away—gave her 2s. But
that is the first money gift she has had since
her confinement a year ago. A lady at a distance, who stayed at the village last year, has
paid for a pint of milk a day for her ever since.

Sometimes the children get " bits " given, but such gifts are quite incalculable.

" They 'ev 'ad nowt lately."

A neighbour, however, brought her a cod's head this week.

Her mother cannot help her much, as the father only earns 15s. a week as a gate opener on the railway. He has five to keep, and the rent is £12 a year.

There is a deficiency of 34 per cent. of protein in this family's dietary, and of 30 per cent. of energy value. One-sixteenth of the food consumed is home produce, and one-fifth is given.

EXPENDITURE DURING TYPICAL WEEK IN OCTOBER 1912.

	s.	d.		s.	d.
1 lb. sugar	0	2	Soap, soda	0	2
½ lb. butter	0	6½	Matches	0	0½
1 cwt. coal	1	3	Paraffin	0	1½
¼ lb. tea	0	4½	Baking powder . . .	0	1¼
1 lb. treacle	0	2½	¼ lb. ground rice . . .	0	0¾
1½ stones flour . . .	2	7½	Rent (weekly) . . .	1	11
2 oz. yeast	0	1½	Tobacco	0	5½
Salt	0	0½	Insurance	0	4
¾ lb. lard	0	5½			
				9	0

HOME PRODUCE CONSUMED DURING THE WEEK.
8 lbs. potatoes. | 7½ lbs. turnips.

GIFTS CONSUMED DURING THE WEEK.
¼ lb. butter.   7 pints whole milk.
1 lb. curds.   Cod's head.

Menu of Meals provided during the Week.

	BREAKFAST.	DINNER.	TEA.	SUPPER.
SUN. .	Tea with milk (no sugar), sad - cakes, c h e e s e-cake, bread and butter.	Turnips and potatoes.	Tea and milk, curd cheese-cake.	Tea, bread and butter, sad-cake.
MON. .	Tea and milk, bread and butter, c h e e s e-cake.	Turnips and potatoes.	Tea and milk, bread and butter, sad - cakes, c h e e s e-cake.	Tea, bread and butter, c h e e s e-cake.
TUES.	Bread and treacle, tea with milk, cheesecake.	Tea, bread and treacle.	Tea, sad-cake and t r e a c l e, cheesecake.	Tea, bread and treacle.
WED.	Tea, bread and treacle, sad - cake and treacle.	Turnips and potatoes.	Tea, bread and treacle.	Tea, bit of dry sad-cake.
THUR.	Tea, milk-p o w d e r cakes.	Cod's head and pota-toes.	Tea, dry p o w d e r cakes.	Tea.
FRI. .	Tea and cakes with butter.	Sad - cakes with butter, tea.	Tea and milk, hot sad-cake and cheese-cake.	None.
SAT. .	Tea and milk, bread and treacle, cheesecake.	Sad - cakes and treacle, tea.	Tea, bread and treacle, curd cheese-cake.	Tea, bread and butter.

On about two days in the week the woman and the little girl have tea and bread and butter between breakfast and dinner.

The children have supper one day in the week (Sunday). The man generally has merely a drink of tea at supper-time, but on Sundays a piece of bread and butter also. The woman has supper fairly regularly.

Study No. XIX.—Oxfordshire.

Man, wife, four sons, aged nine, six, four, and two, and one daughter, aged twelve.

TOTAL WEEKLY EARNINGS OF FAMILY.

	s.	d.
Wages—		
Man	12	0
Wife (from lodger)	3	6
	15	6
Perquisites—		
Milk	1	9
	17	3

Extra earnings in the course of the year, 30s., earned by the woman.

Rent of cottage and garden, 2s. per week.

The family of the Bellamys has suffered pretty heavily from irregularity of employment, due to the uncertain health of the chief breadwinner. The previous year he was out of regular work from February to December, and had only four full weeks during that time, while sometimes he brought home as little as 2s. Fortunately, his wife managed to secure a good place as charwoman, where she earned 10s. weekly; but they still have a few bad debts, which they try to pay off gradually with any extra money earned by either. It would be a great deal easier, however, to accumulate new debts than to pay off old ones. It will be seen in this budget that the expenditure has slightly outrun the income, though there is no apparent extravagance. On such occasions the eldest girl, Emily, who is now earning 3s. 6d. a week, has to lend, if not give, her mother a shilling; but the greater part of her money goes in clothing, and, as a rule, she can only afford to treat her younger brothers and sisters to a few sweets on Sunday

They buy their groceries at the Co-operative Stores, and a kindly neighbour, who is better off than Mrs. Bellamy, gives the latter her checks. The united dividends amount to £1, 6s. for the half-year, and this buys shoes for the whole family, and helps with any arrears of rent, etc. Then the village is fortunate in the matter of jumble sales. Two are held in the year, which the Bellamys attend with alacrity, and which supply them with the bulk of their clothing.

A little more help comes in the summer, when Mrs. Bellamy does charing for summer visitors, at the rate of 5s. weekly, for about six weeks.

Part of the money thus earned is spent on sugar. She has currants and apples and gooseberries in the garden, and blackberries are always to be gathered in the autumn; and she makes a quantity of jam, which they use in the winter, at the rate of about 2 lbs. weekly.

Mr. Bellamy walks five miles and back on Saturdays, that he may buy the meat and groceries rather more cheaply in the market of the nearest large town. His work lately has been pretty regular; but a man who has once suffered from epileptic fits has more than his share of anxiety concerning the future.

They are lucky in having a lodger, whose 3s. 6d. a week—3s. for lodging and 6d. for washing— is a most valuable asset. It means more crowding, as there are only two bedrooms; but the baby and the little girl sleep with Mr. and Mrs. Bellamy, and the boys sleep with the lodger. The latter gets all his food out.

They are beginning just now to look forward sadly to the end of the potatoes, which, used at the rate of about 4 lbs. daily, will only last till the end of January.

There is a deficiency of 21 per cent. of protein

in this family's dietary, and of 11 per cent. of
energy value. One-ninth of the food consumed
is home produce, and one-eleventh is a perquisite.

EXPENDITURE DURING TYPICAL WEEK IN DECEMBER 1912.

	s.	d.		s.	d.
4 lbs. flour	0	6	½ lb. cheese	0	4
4 bloaters	0	3	1½ cwt. coal	1	9
¼ lb. rice	0	0½	Oil, candles, matches	0	4
1 lb. Quaker oats	0	3	2 oz. tobacco	0	7
4 lbs. sugar	0	8	Rent	2	0
½ lb. tea	0	8	Insurance	0	3
2 oz. cocoa	0	2	Soap, soda	0	2
½ lb. lard	0	4½	Wood	0	2
1 lb. margarine	0	8			
2 oz. currants	0	0½		15	1
2½ lbs. neck of beef	1	3	Balance towards debts	0	5
Bullock's heart	0	6			
36 lbs. bread	4	1½		15	6

HOME PRODUCE CONSUMED DURING THE WEEK.

28 lbs. potatoes.   ½ lb. onions.
8 lbs. cabbage.   2 lbs. apples.
2 lbs. jam.

PERQUISITES CONSUMED DURING THE WEEK.
14 pints skim milk.

GIFTS CONSUMED DURING THE WEEK.
2 eggs.

	BREAKFAST.	DINNER.	TEA.	SUPPER.
Sun. .	Tea, porridge, bread and lard.	Roast beef, potatoes, cabbage, apple pie.	Tea, bread and margarine, cake.	Cocoa, bread and lard.
Mon. .	Tea, porridge, bread and lard.	Cold beef, potatoes and cold cabbage.	Tea, bread and jam.	Cocoa, bread and margarine.
Tues. .	Tea, porridge, bread and margarine.	Potatoes and onions made into pie, bread and margarine.	Tea, bread and margarine or jam.	Cocoa, bread and jam.
Wed. .	Tea, bread and margarine.	Bullock's heart, potatoes, cabbage, rice pudding.	Tea, bread and jam.	Remainder of rice pudding.
Thur. .	Tea, bread and jam.	Remainder of heart, potatoes, bread pudding.	Tea, bread and jam, remainder of bread pudding.	Bread and cheese.
Fri. .	Tea, bread and jam or margarine.	Potatoes, bread and jam.	Tea, bloaters, bread and jam.	Bread and cheese.
Sat. .	Tea, bread and jam.	Bread and cheese.	Tea, bread and jam.	Bread and lard.

Only the man and wife take supper, but occasionally one of the children has " a snack."

Some days the woman has a little bread and lard or jam between breakfast and dinner.

Study No. XX.—North Riding of Yorkshire.

Man, wife, son aged twelve, nephew aged eight, and daughter aged nine.

TOTAL WEEKLY EARNINGS OF FAMILY.

Wages—		s.	d.
Man		17	0
Wife		0	4½
		17	4½

No extra earnings.
Rent of cottage and garden, £5 per year.
Rent of common land share, 5s. per year.

Mrs. Smith is a woman whose apron might be cleaner, and who, her neighbours say, is quite inadequate in the sphere of patching and mending and remaking, but who, nevertheless, is struggling hard and pluckily. Her husband has 17s. a week all the year round. He would only be getting 15s., but that he works on Sundays, attending to cattle, generally from 6 a.m. to 8 a.m., and then from 1 p.m. to 4 p.m. Probably his beer is paid for by occasional odd jobs in the village, but we have set down what is the limit of his expenditure on it in the week.

There is no extra money, and there are no perquisites except a few cabbages or turnips. He brings these home every other day when they are in season. The rent for the four-roomed cottage is £5, and has to be put by each week. Their garden is small, and has only yielded them potatoes for three months this year; and the hay on their " common share," for which they pay 5s. yearly, has all been bad.

She herself earns 1s. 6d. about once a month, but she cannot undertake much outside work. There are three children to look after, two of her own and one of her brother's, and she is expecting another child.

Last year her husband was very ill, and a specialist was sent for; and there is a doctor's bill of six guineas against them. They try to set aside a few pence every week towards it, but do not always succeed.

The brother whose little boy they keep is a widower, who is only earning 15s., and has to pay 5s. weekly for the board and lodging of his other child elsewhere, and he gives his sister nothing.

Smith sometimes gets a cast-off coat given, and occasionally old clothing is given to the woman; but all the shoes must be bought.

The expenditure varies very little from week to week. It will be noted that in the budget given it somewhat outruns the settled income. But occasionally, though not often, the man gets some bit of work in the village, and earns an additional shilling. And it is very probable that the family is slightly in debt.

There is a deficiency of 19 per cent. of protein in this family's dietary, and of 2 per cent. of energy value. One per cent. of the food consumed is a perquisite.

EXPENDITURE DURING TYPICAL WEEK IN DECEMBER 1912.

	s.	d.		s.	d.
3¼ lbs. stewing steak .	2	0	Rent and rates . . .	2	3
2 stones flour . . .	3	3	2 cwt. coal	2	8
2 stones potatoes. . .	1	4	2 oz. tobacco	0	7
Baking powder and yeast	0	2½	Insurance	0	4
4 lbs. sugar	0	10	¼ lb. cheese	0	2½
½ lb. butter	0	7½	1 lb. sausages . . .	0	7
1 quart oil, and candles .	0	6	4⅔ pints new milk . .	0	7
½ lb. lard	0	4	Beer	0	3
6 oz. tea	0	6			
2¼ lbs. dripping * . .	0	8		17	8½

* Bought cheaply of employer.

HOME PRODUCE CONSUMED DURING THE WEEK.
½ lb. onions.

GIFTS CONSUMED DURING THE WEEK.
¼ stone apples (windfalls, begged from a neighbour).
4 lbs. cabbage.   4 lbs. turnips.

MENU OF MEALS PROVIDED DURING THE WEEK.

	BREAKFAST.	DINNER.	TEA.	SUPPER.
SUN. .	Tea, fried meat and fresh bread cakes.	Meat pie, potatoes, greens.	Tea, bread and butter or dripping, apple pastry.	None.
MON. .	Tea, bread and butter.	Remainder of Sunday's meat pie (for man), pastry, tea.	Tea, bread and butter or dripping, pastry.	None.
TUES. .	Tea, bread and butter or dripping.	Roast beef, greens, potatoes, tea.	Tea, bread and butter or dripping, pastry.	"Drink of tea."
WED. .	Tea, bread and butter or dripping.	Beef pie (for man), a little stew, potatoes, onions.	Tea, bread and butter or dripping.	None.
THUR. .	Tea, bread and butter or dripping.	Remainder of beef pie and bread and cheese (for man), rest of stew with potatoes and onions, tea.	Tea, bread and butter or dripping.	Tea, bread and cheese.
FRI. .	Tea, bread and dripping.	Sausages, potatoes, tea, bread and cheese (man).	Tea, bread and dripping, pastry.	None.
SAT. .	Tea, bread and dripping.	Sausages, potatoes, swedes.	Tea, bread and butter or dripping, pastry.	None.

Study No. XXI.—North Riding of Yorkshire.

Man, wife; three sons, aged six, four, and four months; and one daughter, aged eight.

TOTAL WEEKLY EARNINGS OF FAMILY.

	s.	d.
Man's wage	17	0
Perquisites—		
Milk, say	0	10½
	17	10½

No extra earnings.

Rent of cottage and garden, £3 per year; rates, 12s. 6d. per year.

The Walpoles are a cordial, friendly couple, who are quite willing to tend the right hand of fellowship to any chance visitor. When we went, Walpole was at home with a sprained wrist, and Mrs. Walpole was nursing the baby, with whom she had been up all night; but they were both invincibly cheery. The wife, handsome, black-haired, and rosy-cheeked, kept the small living-room beautifully clean, and there were cakes of bread rising on the fender.

The cottage is a tiny one, which, under its roof of thatch, looks rather like a small face under a mushroom hat. They told us that the thatch on one side of the cottage actually touched the ground. It contains, however, four small rooms, the two bedrooms being " tucked away in the roof." It is rather dark, and looks more pictur-esque than healthy. The garden in front is merely a square yard or two; there is a fair-sized one behind, but for the greater part of the year they have to buy their potatoes. Some gooseberry bushes, however, are a great asset when the time for making jam comes.

Two of the four children were out playing when we called, and another, a little boy of four, was lying on the sofa " with a headache." He looked flushed and feverish. None of them are very strong, and Mrs. Walpole told us that she believed the average weekly expenditure on medicine would amount to threepence. But Mr. Walpole interpolated, " Say a penny!" and so we left it at the latter figure. At all events only this week they have had to keep a fire burning day and night, and this involves an additional expenditure on coal, which is left out of the budget as being exceptional.

Walpole works at a regular wage of 17s. weekly and three pints of old milk daily; and the cottage is £3 yearly. Rates are about 12s. 6d. yearly. He is what his wife calls a " beast-man," and goes three times on Sundays to look after his charge. There is no additional money payment whatever, but at harvest they get a ton of coals. They also get wood enough to last the year.

" Anything at Christmas ? " we suggested.

" A quarter of a pound of baccy," said Mr. Walpole, with a broad grin.

" It isn't what you would call a living, only a sort of putting on," was his verdict on the life. Any pleasure or luxury is barred. The greatest event of the past year was Mr. Walpole's visit to a fat cattle show. On this occasion he got two shillings from his employer, as well as a ticket of admission, and had an enjoyable day. But such purple patches are extremely rare in the life of the Walpoles.

As will be seen on a perusal of the budget, the weekly 17s. all goes on current expenses.

" We get the clothes out of the pigs, or we should never have any."

" What pigs ? "

Then came the story of how, now four years ago, Walpole's brother had given him a " reckling "—in other words, an abnormally small and fragile pig, which could only live if an abnormal amount of care and attention were given to it. This care the Walpoles gladly bestowed, and they succeeded with much difficulty in rearing the puny animal. They kept it for six months, then sold it, and bought two young pigs. By keeping two pigs for six months and selling them before the fattening time they make, to name the very outside figure, £4 yearly. Perhaps, to take the average of the years, £3, 10s. would be nearer the mark. But whatever they make is devoted to clothing for the whole family. No entry is made in the budget for the keep of these pigs, which live mainly on " the children's scraps," cabbages, and bad potatoes.

Walpole does not come back to dinner, but takes some bread and meat with him. His work is a mile away, and he has to be there at 6.30 a.m.

Potatoes are bought at the rate of a stone a week, and " you can always beg a turnip." Pressed as to the meaning of " always," it turned out to mean occasionally. In this budget, however, they are credited with one good-sized turnip. They beg them when a laden cart is going by.

Very occasionally, too, they get a rabbit given. The wife and the children hardly ever touch meat.

The chief extravagance of this family is a half-penny evening paper. The husband and wife are both quick, intelligent people, who want to see better times. Like most of our other informants, they gave all the facts for which we asked most willingly, and with no thought of any compensation, simply because they hoped that more complete knowledge of the facts of a labourer's life might make things better for the rising generation, if not for them.

Walpole was emphatic on the need for a " Labourers' Union."

" Nothing can ever be done unless they combine. And it's for the north country to set the example."

He thought that in the south country the labourer was too much depressed to set an example to any one.

The relations between him and his employer were quite cordial. His wage was regular, and he even got an occasional day at his own garden without having it docked.

The wife expatiated on the superiority of old milk to separated milk, saying, " If you leave it overnight, you can get a fresh cream in the morning." A good deal of this milk is used with cocoa. The children have cocoa for breakfast, made three parts with milk. Mrs. Walpole takes it at supper with porridge, and at least once a week there is a large milk pudding.

There is a deficiency of 11 per cent. of protein in this family's dietary, and of 5 per cent. of energy value. One-seventh of the food consumed is a perquisite.

EXPENDITURE DURING TYPICAL WEEK IN MARCH 1913.

	s.	d.		s.	d.
2 stones flour	3	4	¼ lb. tea	0	4½
3 lbs. sugar	0	7	⅓ lb. onions	0	0½
1 lb. butter	1	4	1 egg	0	1
Yeast and baking powder	0	4	6 oz. rice	0	1
1 stone potatoes . . .	0	6	2 oz. tobacco	0	7
2½ lbs. golden syrup . .	0	7½	Club and insurance . .	0	7
1½ cwt. coal	1	8	Newspapers	0	3
½ lb. lard	0	3½	Rent and rates . . .	1	4½
¼ lb. cocoa	0	4½	1 lb. soap, blue, etc. . .	0	3½
1 lb. Quaker oats . .	0	3	Oil, candles, matches .	0	4
1 lb. brawn	0	7	Medicine	0	1
½ lb. liver	0	2			
5 lbs. beef and ¼ lb. suet	2	8½		17	0
½ lb. currants . . .	0	2			

HOME PRODUCE CONSUMED DURING THE WEEK.
2 lbs. jam.

PERQUISITES CONSUMED DURING THE WEEK.
21 pints old milk.

GIFT CONSUMED DURING THE WEEK.
2 lbs. turnips.

	BREAKFAST.	DINNER.	TEA.	SUPPER.
SUN. .	Tea, cocoa, bread and butter or syrup, fried meat (man).	Roast beef, Yorkshire pudding, potatoes, turnip.	Tea, bread and butter or syrup, cake, jam pastry.	Porridge (for woman), tea and cake (for man).
MON.	Tea, cocoa, bread and butter or syrup, meat (for man).	Tea, bread and syrup.	Tea, meat (for man), bread and butter or syrup, cake.	Porridge (for woman).
TUES.	Tea, cocoa, bread and butter or syrup, meat (for man).	Tea, bread and butter or syrup.	Tea, cold meat, potatoes, suet dumplings eaten with syrup.	Porridge (for woman).
WED.	Tea, cocoa, bread and butter or syrup, meat (for man).	Tea, bread and butter or syrup.	Tea, hash with potatoes and onion, currant dumpling.	Porridge (for woman).
THUR.	Tea, cocoa, bread and butter or syrup, meat (for man).	Tea, bread and butter or syrup.	Tea, fried liver, potatoes, bread and butter or syrup, pastry.	Porridge (for woman).
FRI. .	Tea, cocoa, bread and butter or syrup, brawn (for man).	Tea, bread and butter or syrup.	Tea, brawn (for man), rice pudding, bread and syrup, pastry.	Porridge (for woman).
SAT. .	Tea, cocoa, bread and butter or syrup, brawn (for man).	Tea, bread and butter or syrup, pie.	Tea, brawn (for man), bread and butter or syrup, pastry.	Porridge (for woman).

Each day the man takes bread and meat or bread and brawn with him for dinner.

Study No. XXII.—East Riding of Yorkshire.

Man, wife, two sons, aged five and three.

TOTAL WEEKLY EARNINGS OF FAMILY.

	s.	d.
Man's wage	18	0

No extra earnings.
Rent of cottage, 2s. 8d. per week.
Rent of allotment, 1s. 6d. per year.

Mrs. Metcalfe is a brisk, alert little woman, yet the presence of two young and extremely active children in the house prevents her from keeping it in apple-pie order. She lives in a small court, in a two-roomed cottage whose rent is 2s. 8d. weekly. There was some difficulty in getting a quiet discussion, since the two children swarmed round their mother, giving a general effect of a much larger number; but when Georgie had been sent for " goo-goos," and Jimmy had been persuaded to " go and play with Algernon," another small boy belonging to the court, the household budget was forthcoming.

Mr. Metcalfe, a quiet, reliable man of thirty, shy and kindly, is at present working for the village joiner and undertaker at 18s. a week. The chief details of the budget had been supplied before it transpired that at the moment he could only ironically be described as working on the land. But as the industry of " coffin-making " was obviously rural as well as urban, it was thought better to complete the budget and description, especially as the wage was the same as that given by the neighbouring farmers, and the parish was purely rural. Moreover, most of Metcalfe's work since they came to the village has been wholly agricultural, and the recent change in his occupation has not altered his mode of living.

Hitherto Mrs. Metcalfe has managed to keep out of debt completely, although the income allows of no extravagance. The house is in a village, but has no garden, and every potato has to be bought ; a turnip, as a rule, can be begged from one or other of the farmers, who are " very kind if you ask."

But Mrs. Metcalfe is rather an independent little woman, and any garden produce that she begs may be regarded as a negligible quantity. Meanwhile they have, with a good deal of difficulty, secured an allotment—half a rood at 1s. 6d. per year.

Metcalfe gives his wife only 15s. weekly. But she is quite content with this arrangement, for out of the remaining 3s. he pays his club and insurance contributions and all his personal expenses. She herself has begun to pay into a clothing club.

The winter before last they had a rough time, as he could not get regular work for six months, but even then they never got into debt.

" He always brought home enough to get flour, and we went short of other things," says the wife.

So far they find the coffin industry rather more satisfactory than was the work with farmers; though there is no overtime money, the pay is pretty regular. Metcalfe's master employs him in his garden when the joinering is slack.

As a rule, firewood is picked up.

There is a deficiency of 21 per cent. of protein in this family's dietary; 0·7 per cent. of the food consumed was given.

EXPENDITURE DURING TYPICAL WEEK IN JANUARY 1913.

	s.	d.		s.	d.
1½ stones flour . . .	2	6	2 oz. baking powder . .	0	1½
1 lb. margarine . . .	0	6	½ lb. sausages . . .	0	3½
½ lb. lard	0	4	Rent	2	8
1 cooking egg . . .	0	1	1 lb. soap	0	3
½ lb. dripping . . .	0	2½	Oil, candles, matches .	0	3
½ lb. tea	0	7	1 cwt. coal	1	4
2 pints new milk . .	0	3	Carrier	0	1
Fish and chips . . .	0	3	Clothing club	0	6
1 stone potatoes . . .	0	6	Kept by the man for		
3 lbs. loin pork and 2 oz.			insurance, club, cloth-		
suet	2	0	ing	3	0
1 lb. liver	0	4			
2 lbs. jam	0	7½		17	8
4 lbs. sugar	0	8	Balance towards clothing	0	4
3 oz. yeast	0	2			
½ lb. currants . . .	0	2		18	0

GIFTS CONSUMED DURING THE WEEK.

3 lbs. turnips.

MENU OF MEALS PROVIDED DURING THE WEEK.

	BREAKFAST.	DINNER.	TEA.	SUPPER.
SUN. .	Tea, sausages and bread.	Roast pork, Yorkshire pudding, potatoes, tea.	Tea, bread and margarine or jam, pastry.	Tea, bread, pastry.
MON. .	Tea, bread and margarine or dripping.	Cold pork, potatoes, pastry.	Tea, bread and margarine or jam, pastry.	Tea.
TUES. .	Tea, bread and margarine or dripping.	Fried pork (for man), baked potatoes and turnips, pastry.	Tea, bread and margarine, pastry.	Tea.
WED. .	Tea, bread and margarine or dripping or jam.	Hashed meat with potatoes, pastry, tea.	Tea, bread and margarine, pastry.	Tea.
THUR. .	Tea, bread and margarine or dripping or jam.	Fried liver and suet dumplings, potatoes, pastry, tea.	Tea, bread and margarine or jam, pastry.	Tea.
FRI. .	Tea, bread and margarine or dripping.	Remainder of liver with potatoes, pastry, tea.	Tea, bread and margarine, pastry.	None.
SAT. .	Tea, bread and margarine.	Fish and chips, pastry, tea.	Tea, bread and margarine or jam, pastry.	Tea and pastry.

The man and wife have a little supper, very often only a drink of tea.

Study No. XXIII.—Oxfordshire.

Woman, two sons, aged twenty and sixteen, and two daughters, aged fourteen and eleven.

TOTAL WEEKLY EARNINGS OF FAMILY.

Wages—	s.	d.
Woman	0	7
Son	8	6
Son	7	0
Daughter	2	0
	18	1

No extra earnings.
Rent of cottage, £4, 2s. 6d. per year.
Rent of allotment, 12s. per year.

Mrs. Jackson has been a widow for eleven years. She was left at her husband's death with six children, one an infant, and somehow or other, with the help of the parish, she pulled through. Many a time she went out to do a day's work, and came back tired and hungry, bringing with her for the children at home the food she ought to have eaten herself; and then she has started work again to earn a few pence by washing.

" Didn't you get pretty downhearted sometimes ? "

" Despair wasn't in it ; I've wanted to die and be out of it all."

But instead of dying she brought up her family to be healthy, self-respecting, and as happy as most people. The eldest son is a soldier in India ; the eldest daughter is married, and though poorly off, she took in one of her brothers last year when he had the influenza, till he regained strength.

There are four children at home, all under twenty-one. The eldest son earns 8s. 6d. a week, the second son 7s. Mrs. Jackson's own earnings average about 7d. (6¾d., to be strictly correct) a week. She is often kept waiting week after week for money due. The third child, a girl of fourteen, earns 2s. a week, and gets her dinner out. She has breakfast before she goes, arriving at her post soon after seven, and comes home between three and four. The youngest child, a girl, is at school. Mrs. Jackson's own mother, herself poorly off, and in receipt of the old age pension, sometimes helps a little with this child's clothes.

The rent is £4, 2s. 6d., for a house with four small rooms and hardly any garden—a very tiny square in front. They get all their vegetables from their allotment, ¼ acre, which costs 12s. a year. Last year seed potatoes alone cost them 7s. The young fellows work at it in the evenings, " instead of pleasure," as they sometimes say ruefully. Yet there is a certain amount of pleasure in their lives, though they have even run out of the subscriptions to the football club. In winter the evenings are cheery. They do not go to the reading-room, with its weekly fee; but other lads sometimes come in, and have a game of cards. Probably by nine o'clock, however, all are asleep. Francis, the eldest, often has been known to go to bed at seven. But, as a rule, they have some kind of scratch supper about eight.

The quality and quantity of the food leave much to be desired.

" The boys often come home hungry," says the mother, " and there's nothing but potatoes and a little margarine."

Meat for breakfast is unknown. The times when they get back for dinner vary, and sometimes the chief meal of the day is at noon, sometimes at teatime. Mrs. Jackson calculates that she uses about a quarter of a peck of potatoes a

day—five sacks lasting ten months. They have
greens or turnips or carrots twice a week, and use
a good many onions in the winter.

The main diet is potatoes, bread, and margarine.

" What do you call it butter for ? " says Joseph, the second lad, to his mother. " Why
can't you say margarine and have done with it ? "

" Oh, I don't know," replies Mrs. Jackson.
" Butter sounds higher."

She is a woman with a fine, sad face, who looks
as if all the waves and storms of this world had
gone over her, though she is not an unhappy
woman. These people who rough it very often
get a curious faith in some kind of overruling
wisdom. But when she sees her children go
without the little pleasures other children have,
or without adequate food, she becomes resentful.

" Then I'm done," she says. And after a
pause, " I sometimes wonder whether the rich
people who sit down to six or seven courses ever
think about a working boy."

Asked her idea of a minimum wage for the
labourer with a family, Mrs. Jackson promptly
said, " A pound." That is the uniform answer

from the people who are living on so much less. They know that less means insufficient food and dependence on charity for at least most of their clothing.

" But of course we shall never get that," she added.

She did not want riches; none of these people do. But they want to be able to feed and clothe their children comfortably and decently.

" When I've seen other children with warm clothing, and mine jealous," said Mrs. Jackson, " then I haven't known what to say. I know our Master wasn't rich. We've got a roof to cover us, and He hadn't where to lay His head. So I daresay it's all for the best. But they say English people ought to be strong and brave, and I don't know how they *expect* them, living as they do, to be strong and brave and cheerful ! "

" There will be better times, even if we don't see them."

Mrs. Jackson's face lit up. " Yes, maybe our children will see them."

The budget given for the week is fairly typical. The elder son earns a little overtime in the year. It is not much (his mother did not know the exact sum), and he does not give it to her. Shoes and clothing doubtless absorb it.

The amount set aside for clothing in this budget is pretty representative, as at other times there will be shirting, or calico, or dress material, or more shoes to buy. They get very little help from outside, as now that two sons and a daughter are working, they are considered comparatively well off.

There is a deficiency of 18 per cent. of protein in this family's dietary, and of 9 per cent. of energy value. One-tenth of the food consumed is home produce.

EXPENDITURE DURING TYPICAL WEEK IN NOVEMBER 1912.

	s.	d.		s.	d.
43 lbs. bread	5	0½	2½ pints milk	0	3½
1 lb. rice	0	2	Blacking	0	1
¼ stone flour	0	5½	Newspaper, daily	0	3
4 lbs. sugar	0	8	Laces, cotton	0	1
6 oz. tea	0	6	Eldest son's pocket-		
8 kippers	0	6	money	1	0
1 lb. cheese	0	9	Insurance for two	0	8
2 lbs. chilled meat (steak)	1	0	Instalment towards shoes		
¼ lb. suet	0	1½	just bought for second		
Oil, candles, matches	0	3½	son	0	6
Soap and starch	0	3½	Instalment towards coat		
Coal	1	3	for girl	1	0
Rent	1	6			
Allotment rent	0	3		18	0
1½ lbs. margarine	1	0			
½ lb. corned beef	0	4			

24½ lbs. potatoes. | 6 lbs. turnips.
3 lbs. savoys. | 1 lb. onions.

MENU OF MEALS PROVIDED DURING THE WEEK.

	BREAKFAST.	DINNER.	TEA.	SUPPER.
SUN. .	Tea, bread and margarine.	Roast meat, potatoes, greens, suet dumplings.	Tea, bread and margarine.	Bread and cheese.
MON. .	Tea, bread and margarine.	Cold meat, mashed potatoes.	Tea, bread and margarine.	Bread and cheese or margarine.
TUES. .	Tea, bread and margarine.	Remains of meat stewed with onions, potatoes, rice, bread.	Tea, bread and margarine.	Bread and cheese or margarine.
WED. .	Tea, bread and margarine.	Soup (made with rice), suet pudding, turnips, potatoes.	Tea, bread and margarine.	None.
THUR. .	Tea, bread and margarine.	Corned beef, potatoes, turnips.	Tea, bread and margarine.	None.
FRI. .	Tea, bread and margarine.	Kippers, potatoes.	Tea, bread and margarine.	"A drink of tea."
SAT. .	Tea, bread and margarine.	Fried potatoes, bread and margarine.	Tea, bread and margarine.	Tea, bread and margarine.

When not at home for dinner in the middle of the day, the sons often take bread and cheese.

Study No. XXIV.—Essex.

Man, wife, two sons aged thirteen and ten, and three daughters aged fourteen, seven, and four months.

TOTAL WEEKLY EARNINGS OF FAMILY.

Wages—		*s.*	*d.*
Man		15	0
Son		1	3
		16	3
Perquisites—			
Cottage and garden, say . .		2	0
		18	3

Extra earnings in the course of the year, £1, 5s.

The Pratts are labouring people of a fine type. The man is not much over thirty, a dark, good-looking fellow; the woman is small and fair, and full of nervous energy, keeping her house and children beautifully neat and clean.

Pratt's regular wage is 15s., and they have the cottage free. He works from 5 a.m. to 5.30 p.m., with half-an-hour for breakfast and an hour for dinner, or whatever the eleven o'clock meal to which he returns is called. The children take something to school with them, and they all have " high tea " together at 6 p.m., or rather earlier.

Pratt only gives his wife 13s. Out of the remaining 2s. his insurance is deducted, and he buys a newspaper, and one ounce of tobacco, and generally a pint of beer on Saturday or Sunday. He is supposed likewise to be responsible for his own clothing.

The additional harvest money works out at £1 ; the hay-making this year did not bring him in more than 5s. extra. These sums are relied upon to provide clothing ; but it must not be forgotten that overtime money invariably means increased expenditure on food.

The eldest boy, Noel, will soon have left school. Meanwhile he is earning 1s. 3d. a week and his breakfast. He works hard for it, going to the rectory to clean knives, boots, and the like, at 7.30 every morning, before 9 o'clock school. At 4 p.m. he goes back, and works again for about an hour and a half. On Saturdays he goes for the whole day, and on Sundays he goes in the morning for about two hours. The 1s. is put aside regularly out of his wage by his mother to pay for his clothing, and the threepence is absorbed in the general expenditure.

When this budget was taken, in the beginning

of December, the family was still using potatoes from the garden ; but the supply was just exhausted, and Mrs. Pratt told us that she would have to buy in a few days, and would then begin to use them at the rate of a stone a week. The additional expense would be met by reducing bread and margarine.

Most of the wood is picked up, but this winter they must buy a little.

Half a pound of tea a week may seem extravagant ; but they drink it at most of their meals ; and Pratt has a cup before he goes out at 5 a.m. The rest of the expenditure could hardly be reduced.

The eldest girl, aged fourteen, is still at home helping her mother. She is a sweet-faced but distinctly anæmic-looking girl. Next year, probably, both she and her brother will have found situations. But Mr. Pratt is determined that the girl shall not go very far away from home till she is a good deal older, even if it means an additional drain on the exchequer for some time to come.

In the budget it will be noted that the meat is religiously set aside for the breadwinner. The pastry mentioned as a gift was given to the younger children when they went for the milk to a neighbouring farmer's wife. The farmer's wife in question was reported in the village to be one who " never gave a drop over," and it was maliciously surmised that the pastry must have been " very old and dry." The eight ounces, by all accounts, is probably an over-estimate; but we gave the donor the benefit of the doubt!

There is a deficiency of 36 per cent. of protein in this family's dietary, and of 18 per cent. of energy value. One-twelfth of the food consumed is home produce.

EXPENDITURE DURING TYPICAL WEEK IN DECEMBER 1912.

	s.	d.		s.	d.
½ stone flour	1	0	Oil and candles . . .	0	4
40 lbs. bread	4	7	Soap, blue, starch . .	0	3
1½ lbs. margarine . .	1	0	1 oz. tobacco	0	3½
1 lb. bacon	0	9	Man's pocket money, including insurance and clothes	2	0
6 lbs. sugar	1	0			
½ lb. tea	0	9			
1½ lbs. stewing beef and ½ lb. suet	1	0	Payment on boy's suit .	1	0
1¼ cwt. coal	1	8		16	0
Baking powder and matches.	0	1½	Balance	0	3
1½ pints new milk . .	0	3		16	3

HOME PRODUCE CONSUMED DURING THE WEEK.
15½ lbs. potatoes. | 12½ lbs. savoys.
3 lbs. parsnips.

GIFTS CONSUMED DURING THE WEEK.
8 oz. pastry.

Menu of Meals provided during the Week.

	Breakfast.	Dinner.	Tea.
Sun. . . .	Tea, bacon for the man, bread and dripping or margarine for others.	Potatoes, cabbage, meat in suet pudding.	Tea, bread and margarine, pastry.
Mon. . .	Tea, bread and margarine.	Scrap of meat left from Sunday, with vegetables fried up (man), bread and margarine, tea.	Tea, scrap of meat (for man), potatoes, cabbage.
Tues. . .	Tea, bread and margarine.	Bacon and bread (for man), bread and margarine.	Tea, bacon for man, suet pudding, potatoes, cabbage.
Wed. . .	Tea, bread and margarine.	Bacon (for man), potatoes fried up, bread and margarine, tea.	Tea, suet pudding, potatoes, parsnips, bread and margarine.
Thur. . .	Tea, bread and margarine.	Scrap of bacon (for man), fried parsnips, bread and margarine, tea.	Tea, pudding made with scrap of fat from meat, parsnips, potatoes, bread.
Fri. . . .	Tea, bread and margarine.	Scrap of bacon (for man), parsnips fried up, bread and margarine, tea.	Tea, bread and margarine, potatoes, cabbage.
Sat. . . .	Tea, bread and margarine.	Bread and scrape, tea.	Scrap of meat made into pudding (for man), greens, bread and margarine.

The man has a drink of tea at 5 a.m. each morning. The children take bread and margarine with them to school for dinner. There is no supper.

Study No. XXV.—East Riding of Yorkshire.

Man, wife, three sons aged ten, three, and one and a half, and four daughters aged twelve, eight, seven, and five.

TOTAL WEEKLY EARNINGS OF FAMILY.

	s.	d.
Man's wage	15	0
Perquisites—		
Cottage and garden, milk and potatoes, say	3	7
	18	7

Extra earnings in the course of the year, £2, 12s. (£2 by the man and 12s. by the woman).

Mrs. Mellor is not by any means the best type of labourer's wife. And yet it seemed worth while to get some idea of the manner in which she tried to make both ends meet.

She does not look like a country woman born and bred; nor is she. She and her husband came into the country from the town some years ago. He is a steady and hard-working fellow, with hair of the colour popularly supposed to accompany a hot temper. Probably his wife sometimes irritates him by what the neighbours call her " shiftless ways." Her natural tendency is to exhaust the stores for the week prematurely, and then live in a state of semi-starvation till pay-day comes again. But she has a very practical neighbour, a cousin twice removed, who persistently gives her good counsel, and for the last year or two she really has been trying to " even the food out." Nor is she in debt to any grave extent, though this is chiefly, one fears, because of the sagacity of the trades-men with whom she deals.

Both she and her husband felt some vague discomfort at the idea of furnishing a budget, thinking that it might possibly displease their employer, who took a keen and kindly interest in whatever affected his labourers. But the farmer, on being appealed to, willingly gave us leave to get every item of information that we could from any of his people as to how their incomes were spent. He obviously did not think that Mrs. Mellor's budget would be very illuminating, having himself given considerable attention to the problem of " keeping her in flour and coal." He had done what very few employers would trouble to do, bought in large quantities and actually put her on rations. This was after the discovery that one day she and her children were absolutely without bread.

But he owned that even for a thrifty woman life on the labourer's wage, with nine to keep out of it, was " a hard nut to crack." And when, by dint of perseverance, we arrived at Mrs. Mellor's purchases for the week, and the meals from day to day, she did not seem to have done badly.

There could certainly be improvements. She could, for instance, use more potatoes, as she gets them free, and the farmer would always be willing to give her a couple of turnips. She could get more out of her own garden, with a little time and effort. Yet the budget could hardly be criticized for any extravagance—save, perhaps, the almost inevitable two ounces of tobacco. She shops on Saturday night, walking into a neighbouring town, and bearing her purchases wearily home, rather than paying the carrier, or taking an omnibus, which would save her two miles of the walk. She buys her meat cheap, and keeps a sharp look-out for desirable " bacon shanks." And, after all, we found that the eighteenpenny joint bought the week before had lasted the family three days. For a woman with no natural aptitude for domestic economy that was a pretty fair record. The husband, of course, here as elsewhere, gets most of the meat and bacon.

Probably Mrs. Mellor looks rather more shiftless than she is. When we first interviewed her she had obviously been too busy to wash either her own face or the baby's. And yet a woman who keeps seven children in fairly good health cannot be utterly devoid of practical common sense.

The worst pinch, very probably, is in the clothing bill. Certainly Mr. Mellor gets £2 over - money at harvest. But it is hardly likely that all this sum will be religiously set aside for clothing. If there are no small debts to pay, which have been incurred on the strength of the Michaelmas money, the dietary will assuredly improve for a week or two. As for the 12s. Mrs. Mellor herself earned in the course of the year, part of it had to be used for replacing household utensils.

It is certain that the children are very thinly and poorly clad. No doubt, in a town, Mrs. Mellor would explain her difficulties to one or two comfortable middle-class families, who would put aside all their " casts-offs " for her. But when a woman with young children lives several miles out in the country, begging clothes is not so easy. And in the matter of clothing, just as in the matter of food, the breadwinner has the first claim.

On the whole, we left Mrs. Mellor with a feeling of sympathy. This hard life, with its constant need for thrift, is singularly distasteful to her. Long gossips with intimate friends, and " bought stuff " from the pastrycook's, would be more in her line. Nevertheless she is facing the music.

There is a deficiency of 27 per cent. of protein in this family's dietary, and of 21 per cent. of energy value. One-sixth of the food consumed is a perquisite. Nothing is got from the garden at present.

EXPENDITURE DURING TYPICAL WEEK IN OCTOBER 1912.

	s.	d.		s.	d.
3½ lbs. frozen beef, thin flank, and ½ lb. suet .	1	6	½ lb. liver	0	2
1 egg	0	1	1 lb. rice	0	2
3¼ lbs. bacon shank . .	1	6	½ lb. lard	0	3½
½ lb. tea	0	9	1 lb. soap	0	3
3 lbs. sugar	0	7½	2 oz. tobacco	0	7
¼ lb. yeast	0	2	Coal (every week) . .	2	0
¼ lb. baking powder . .	0	2½	Oil, matches, candles .	0	5
2 lbs. plum jam . . .	0	8½	Cotton, hearthstone, blacking, salt . . .	0	1½
1½ lbs. margarine . .	1	0	Insurance	0	4
2½ stones flour . . .	3	10½			
½ lb. beef sausages . .	0	3		15	0

PERQUISITES CONSUMED DURING THE WEEK.

7 quarts new milk. | 2½ stones potatoes.

MENU OF MEALS PROVIDED DURING THE WEEK.

	BREAKFAST.	DINNER.	TEA.	SUPPER.
SUN. .	Tea, sausages and bread; bread and milk for youngest child every day.	Beef, potatoes, Yorkshire pudding.	Tea, bread, margarine, jam tarts.	Tea, bread and margarine.
MON. ✗.	Tea, bread, boiled bacon shank.	Beef, potatoes, rice pudding.	Tea, bread and margarine.	Tea.
TUES. .	Tea, bacon (for man), bread and margarine.	Hashed beef, potatoes, bread, pastry.	Tea, bread and margarine.	None.
WED. .	Tea, bacon (for man), bread and margarine.	Shank boiled up with potatoes.	Tea, bread and margarine, pastry.	None.
THUR. .	Tea, bread and margarine.	Bread and margarine, pastry, tea.	Tea, bread and margarine, pastry.	None.
FRI. .	Tea, bread and margarine.	Liver, potatoes, suet dumplings.	Tea, bread and margarine, shortcakes.	None.
SAT. .	Tea, bread and margarine.	Rice pudding, bread, tea.	Tea, bread and margarine.	None.

Five of the children take bread and margarine or pastry to school for dinner, and have potatoes at teatime.

Study No. XXVI.—East Riding of Yorkshire.

Man, wife, wife's sister (aged twenty-six), one son aged four, and three daughters aged ten, eight, and six.

TOTAL WEEKLY EARNINGS OF FAMILY.

	s.	d.
Man's wage	17	0
Perquisites—		
Cottage and some potatoes, say . .	2	6
	19	6

Extra earnings in the course of the year, £5, 10s. earned by the woman.

Mr. and Mrs. Woodhead are a very dissimilar couple. He is tall and dark, with a sombre expression; she is of medium height, fair, with a bright though rather delicate colour, and an open, pleasant face. When the purpose of the visit was explained to her, she responded readily.

It was a fairly spacious kitchen, with raftered ceiling, and a bright fire burning in the wide old-fashioned grate. By the fire sat a young woman of perhaps six-and-twenty, with a very attractive face, but a look of ill-health. It was Mrs. Woodhead's youngest sister, who, after breaking down in one situation after another, had come here to rest. She could at present contribute nothing to the household finances, and was simply accepted as one of the family.

There were also four children, well trained, since, while we were present, they succeeded in curbing their impatience to know just what their mother had brought back from the town, four miles away, in which she marketed on Saturdays. They were beautifully neat and clean, as was the living-room, with its large, old-fashioned sofa occupying nearly the whole of one side.

Woodhead earns 17s. a week, and has a free cottage, with potatoes, twenty stones at least, and probably more in a good year. A turnip can always be had for the asking. No milk is allowed, but whenever Woodhead is threshing he gets breakfast, dinner, and tea. This winter he has been threshing two or three days a week, and for the rest of the week there is other employment, as he is a regular hand.

He reserves 2s. for pocket money, out of which he pays his insurance and buys two ounces of tobacco—his wife buys him a third ounce.

Possibly his beer may sometimes amount to a shilling; we did not probe into that detail. Certainly he seems a steady and capable worker. Asked why the agricultural labourers do not form a union, he is very emphatic as to the apathy of the villagers.

" There's no two that's alike. Ivery one on 'em gets fixed in his own orkard way ! They don't *think* about things. . . . If there's any kind of an address i' the place, they'll noan come and hear it."

But it is with farmers that our friend is most annoyed.

" They're the miserablest set of beings on the face of the earth ! "

According to Woodhead, they grow more and more greedy, and more and more indifferent to any hardship among their men. He accounted for this alleged deterioration by their increased love of luxury, excitement, and tea-parties.

" They can't give one of them big tea-parties but it costs 'em five pounds, and that's got to come out of somewhere." Obviously, in the speaker's opinion, it comes out of the labourer's wage.

We quote these remarks because, though few men speak quite so openly, there is very often an undercurrent of similar resentment. In discussing the question of Sunday work, again,

" Shepherds or cattlemen might as well ask for a golden sovereign as for a Sunday off. It's work all the week, and four hours of it on Sunday, if you count the time they take in walking to and fro."

" How do the men like the Insurance Act here ? "

" They don't like it at all. But they're getting the benefits, some on 'em. One fellow swore that he'd have a doctor as soon as New Year came. He'd be all aches and pains. And sure enough, he was the fust to get the benefit —he's getting it now. I'd rather be working myself."

" What does the man's wife say ? For you're worse off even if you do get a benefit."

" Oh, she don't care ! Yon chap drinks all *he* airns ! "

He speaks almost with horror of the idea of condemning his children to a country life.

" They shan't have to work as I've worked."

It is obvious that Woodhead does not really care about the country, but his wife seems happy enough. She lays nothing by during the week for clothing, except sixpence for the clothing club inaugurated by the vicar's wife. But the bulk of the clothing—and they all look comfortably clad—is earned by herself at potato-picking and other field work.

For some work—for example, potato-picking—women get 15s. weekly, but less exhausting work only brings in 2s. a day. She calculates that she must have earned £5 to £5, 10s. in the past twelve months, and could earn more, but that she finds it difficult to leave the children for so long together day after day unless her sister is staying with her. She is now anxious to do a little washing or charing, but says that the village is too poor to have many openings for such work. Apparently very little of what she earns is absorbed by food; at the same time it sets free the regular weekly wage for food and fuel.

She does a great part of her marketing at a neighbouring town, where there is a frozen-meat shop, and cheap remnants suitable for clothing can be picked up. There is a carrier, but she nearly always walks both ways. It is instructive to note that she prefers to walk eight miles rather than spend an unnecessary threepence.

They have no garden. But it is a comfortable four-roomed cottage, that might easily let for half a crown.

They never, or hardly ever, buy bacon, or coffee, or cocoa, or cheese. The funds do not allow it. It is perhaps to their credit, however, that they buy two penny and six halfpenny newspapers every week. Mrs. Woodhead, moreover, contributes—somewhat regretfully, to judge from her intonation—to the collecting box in the chapel they attend.

Vinegar is extremely popular in the Woodhead establishment, and the 2d. entered for it in the budget is typical.

There is a deficiency of 35 per cent. of protein in this family's dietary, and of 26 per cent. of energy value. One-tenth of the food consumed is earned in kind.

	s.	d.		s.	d.
2 stones flour	3	8	2 oz. currants . . .	0	0½
4 oz. yeast	0	2½	½ lb. tea	0	9
Baking powder . . .	0	1½	1½ lbs. soap	0	4½
½ lb. lard	0	4	Man's pocket money, in-		
½ lb. dripping. . . .	0	3	cluding State insur-		
3 lbs. sugar	0	6	ance, tobacco . . .	2	0
1 lb. butter	1	4	Oil and candles . . .	0	4
6 lbs. brisket beef (frozen)			1½ cwt. coal	2	0
and ¼ lb. suet . . .	3	0	1 tin condensed milk .	0	3½
1 lb. sausages (frozen) .	0	5	1 oz. tobacco, news-		
½ lb. curd	0	2	papers	0	8½
1 lb. onions	0	1½			
Vinegar	0	2		16	10
Salt	0	0½			

Balance of 2d., but the weekly payment of 6d. to the Clothing Club is omitted. Probably this is paid partly out of the woman's earnings.

PERQUISITE CONSUMED DURING THE WEEK.

24½ lbs. potatoes.

MENU OF MEALS PROVIDED DURING THE WEEK.

	BREAKFAST.	DINNER.	TEA.
SUN. . . .	Tea, sausages and bread.	Roast beef, potatoes, suet pudding, tea.	Tea, bread and butter, pie.
MON. . . .	Tea, bread and butter.	Cold meat, potatoes, pastry, tea.	Tea, bread and butter or dripping, pie.
TUES. . . .	Tea, bread and butter.	Fried meat, onions, potatoes, pastry.	Tea, bread and butter, pie.
WED. . . .	Tea, bread and butter.	Hashed meat, p o t a t o e s, onions, pastry, tea.	Tea, toast and butter, pie.
THUR. . . .	Tea, bread and butter.	Meat and potato pie, tea.	Tea, bread and butter or dripping.
FRI. . . .	Tea, bread and butter or dripping.	Remainder of potato pie, tea.	Tea, toast and butter, pie.
SAT. . . .	Tea, bread and butter or dripping.	Remainder of cold meat, bread and butter, pastry, tea.	Tea, bread and butter or dripping.

The three adults have supper on Sunday, consisting of tea and fried potatoes. The man had his food out three days during this week. This only happens when he is threshing.

Study No. XXVII.—North Riding of Yorkshire.

Man, wife, three sons, aged nine, five, and three, and one daughter, aged seven.

TOTAL WEEKLY EARNINGS OF FAMILY.

	s.	d.
Man's wage	16	0
Perquisites—		
Cottage, garden, milk, and potatoes, say	3	6
	19	6

Extra earnings in the course of the year, £2.

The Collingwoods live in an unusually large cottage, with four bedrooms and two living-rooms, besides pantry, scullery, and outbuildings. It was once a small farmhouse; they have moved into it from a cottage a hundred yards away, which had become too small for them. At present they only use two of the bedrooms and one living-room; but as the children grow older the other rooms will be pressed into service.

Collingwood gets the cottage free, 16s. a week, free potatoes for the greater part of the year (now being used at the rate of 19 lbs. a week), and a pint of new milk a day. Sometimes they get separated milk also. But this item is variable, as often the supply is exhausted for feeding calves. They thought, however, that it might be set down just at present at three quarts a week. There is £2 harvest money.

Collingwood is a shepherd, and in the summer his hours are from 6 a.m. to 6 p.m. ; but in the winter he goes at about 7. There is Sunday work, heavier in the winter than in the summer ; in the summer he can even accompany his wife to chapel. He is a man of about fifty, very massively built, and with an expression of settled good-humour. At present he is doing some draining for his employer, and wears a pair of high boots which cost 17s., and were bought out of his harvest money.

" You mun have t' best boots when you're all in t' blether," says he, indicating, just below his knee, the depth of mud and water through which he will have to wade.

Mrs. Collingwood is a woman of about forty, rather older in appearance, as her hair is quite grey, though her delicate colour is that of a

young girl. She looks nervous and highly strung
—possibly quick-tempered—but capable to her
finger-tips. There are four children—three boys,
nine, five, and three years old, and a girl of
seven. The mother makes all their clothes
herself, and makes them well, too, buying cheap
but durable materials, or cutting down and remaking. A small brown pair of trousers for the
five-year-old boy is her last achievement. They
were made out of some fragments of a worn-
out suit belonging to his father, and have a
most workmanlike appearance.

Occasionally she earns a shilling by making
some small garment for people in the village;
but, as she felt quite sure that all her earnings
would not work out at 6d. a week, and as they
are so irregular, we have made no attempt to
enter them in the budget. There are five hens,
two of which are laying, and the exact cost of
whose keep it is hard to ascertain. Collingwood says that the " board wage," so to speak,
of a hen which only has a small run is generally
estimated at 3½d. weekly. But his wife adds,
" Where there are bairns there are always some
bits," and these hens live chiefly on " bits " left

by the children. About three eggs are used weekly in the household, and some are sold. Just now they are getting a shilling a week from this source, and hope to make more afterward.

The vegetables grown do not amount to much just yet, as the Collingwoods have only recently moved into this cottage. But there is a good garden, with one or two apple trees, and we may feel pretty sure that they will make the most of it. The allowance of about 40 stones of potatoes is roughly supposed to last nine months in the year, while the garden supplies the other three months. There is, however, no exact measurement.

" When the farmer opens a pie he leaves us a sack." But there is no weighing ; the potatoes are " just poured in," the precise number of stones being regarded as of no significance. On this occasion, however, Mrs. Collingwood weighed the potatoes that she was preparing for dinner for herself, her husband, and the youngest child. There were $1\frac{3}{4}$ lbs. when peeled, and the peel was at least another $\frac{1}{2}$ lb. Another couple of pounds is sometimes cooked later in the day for the three children who lunch at school. Roughly, one may calculate for this family 4½ lbs. of unpeeled potatoes on four days of the week, and half that amount on two days.

Mrs. Collingwood is a first-rate cook, and with the aid of her "home-grown" eggs she turns out a better supply of cakes than most of her neighbours. Her husband likes cakes better than pies or pastry. They have coffee for lunch every day, using ¼ lb. weekly ; and as the present investigators sampled coffee and cakes, and even the " pie " or tart, made with fig and rhubarb jam, they can affirm with confidence that the quality was excellent. The pastry is rather richer than is the rule in such households, since Mrs. Collingwood uses 2 lbs. of lard weekly.

They get what is known as " privilege " butter from the farmer. It is a shilling a pound all the year round.

There is a deficiency of 17 per cent. of protein in this family's dietary. One-sixth of the food consumed is a perquisite.

EXPENDITURE DURING TYPICAL WEEK IN MARCH 1913.

	s.	d.		s.	d.
2 lbs. Quaker oats	0	6	½ lb. liver and 1 lb. pork		
6 oz. tea	0	6	chops	0	10
¼ lb. coffee	0	3	4 lbs. beef and ¼ lb. suet	2	8
1¾ stones flour	3	0	1 lb. ground rice	0	3
Yeast	0	2	1 lb. soap	0	3
¼ lb. baking powder	0	2½	Oil, candles, newspaper	0	5
1 lb. currants	0	4	Food for fowls	0	3
2 lbs. lard	1	2	2 oz. tobacco	0	7
1½ lbs. " privilege " but-			Insurance	0	4
ter	1	6	1½ cwt. coal	2	0
7 lbs. sugar	1	8¼			
½ lb. bacon	0	5		17	3¾

HOME PRODUCE CONSUMED DURING THE WEEK.

3 lbs. jam. | 3 eggs.

2 oz. onions.

PERQUISITES CONSUMED DURING THE WEEK.

7 pints new milk. | 6 pints separated milk.

19 lbs. potatoes.

	Breakfast.	Dinner.	Tea.
Sun. . . .	Tea, fried meat and bread, bread and butter.	Roast beef, potatoes, Yorkshire pudding, currant dumpling, coffee.	Tea, bread and butter, cake, jam, pastry.
Mon. . .	Tea, meat (for man), porridge (for children), bread and butter.	Remainder of Sunday's dinner warmed up, coffee.	Tea, scrap of meat (man), remainder of currant dumpling (for children), bread and butter, cake, pastry.
Tues. . .	Tea, scrap of meat (for man), porridge (for children), bread and butter.	Warmed meat and potatoes (for man), suet dumpling eaten with jam, coffee.	Tea, potatoes and pudding (for children), bread and butter, cake, pastry.
Wed. . .	Tea, scrap of meat (for man), porridge (for children), bread and butter.	Hash, potatoes, pie, cake, coffee.	Tea, bread and butter, remains of hash, cake, pastry.
Thur. . .	Tea, porridge (for children), bread and butter.	Pork chops, potatoes, dumplings with gravy or jam, coffee.	Tea, potatoes and dumplings, scrap of meat, bread and butter, pastry.
Fri. . . .	Tea, cold pork (for man), porridge (for children), bread and butter.	Fried liver and bacon, potatoes, coffee.	Tea, remains of dinner (children), bread and butter, cake, pastry.
Sat. . . .	Tea, scrap of bacon (for man), porridge (children), bread and butter.	Remains of liver and bacon, potatoes, milk pudding (ground rice), coffee.	Tea, bread and butter, cake, pastry.

About once a week the husband and wife have a cup of coffee and piece of cake for supper. The children take cake or pastry with them to school for dinner, and have their share of dinner at teatime.

Study No. XXVIII.—North Riding of Yorkshire.

Man, wife, two sons, aged five and three, and two daughters, aged seven and ten months.

TOTAL WEEKLY EARNINGS OF FAMILY.

	s.	d.
Man's wage	16	0
Perquisites—		
Cottage, garden, milk, and potatoes, say	3	6
	19	6

Extra earnings in the course of the year . . . £2.

The entry to the Murrays' cottage is guarded by a handsome yellow sheep-dog, with a morbid objection to visitors. Not till Mrs. Murray came out and told him to " sit down " three times in succession would he permit us to cross the threshold.

Mrs. Murray looks a mere girl, though she has four children, their ages ranging from seven years to ten months. It was washing-day when we saw her, and she looked somewhat overwhelmed by household cares and the weight of the heavy baby whom she nursed religiously

while she talked, by way of persuading herself
that she was not wasting her time. The baby
looked healthy and extremely substantial; but
she told us that he had suffered through her
being too ill to nurse him. At present, however, he consumes a pint of new milk a day,
and probably a little of whatever else is going.

Mrs. Murray is certainly fragile, and has the
timid, shrinking look of one rather expectant
of bad luck than good. Yet the object of the
inquiry once explained, she was very willing
to tell us exactly how she spent the weekly
income. She has a horror of debt, and this
always means that the winter is an especially
hard struggle, since people imbued with it are
not content to let any arrears accumulate in the
hope of paying them off when there is less expenditure on fuel. As is often the case, she
models her purchases to some extent upon those
of an older woman living close by, whose husband works for the same farmer. Like her, she
also gives her children porridge on six days in
the week, and as a rule she buys the same cut of
beef. But there are trifling differences: she
uses more milk on account of the baby, and hav-

ing no poultry, like her neighbour, and being reluctant to buy eggs, she makes more of her flour into pastry and less into cakes.

Her husband is a cowman, and the tiny four-roomed cottage is free. They also get most of their potatoes and a pint of new milk daily, as well as a varying amount of separated milk. The latter is occasionally made into puddings, or ekes out the new with the porridge and the tea. Nearly all the meat is eaten by the husband. The garden is small, but furnishes its quota of the potatoes, and they are just finishing the sprouts.

When we called, Mr. Murray had driven with some pigs into a large town ten miles away. This meant an extra shilling from the farmer, which would most of it, however, be spent by the man on dinner and tea. Still, it made a variety in the daily routine ; and as it was " the first break for ever so many months," it was welcome.

He is a steady, reliable worker, and though he is fond of a glass of beer, his expenditure on it is almost *nil*.

There is a deficiency of 8 per cent. of protein

in this family's dietary. One per cent. of the food consumed is home produce, and 15 per cent. perquisites.

EXPENDITURE DURING TYPICAL WEEK IN MARCH 1913.

	s.	d.		s.	d.
2 stones flour	3	2	2 lbs. Quaker oats	0	6
Yeast	0	2	1 lb. sausages	0	6
Baking powder	0	2	¾ lb. pork chops	0	6
1 lb. butter	1	0	½ lb. rice	0	1
5 lbs. sugar	0	11½	Insurance	0	4
Salt and pepper	0	0½	Tobacco	0	6
2 lbs. lard	1	2	Newspaper	0	1
1 lb. currants	0	4	1 lb. soap	0	3
7 pints new milk	0	10½	Coal and wood	1	6
2 lbs. beef and ¼ lb. suet	1	4	Oil, candles, matches	0	4
3 lbs. bacon (shoulder) largely bone	1	6		16	0½
½ lb. tea	0	9			

PERQUISITES CONSUMED DURING THE WEEK.

7 pints new milk. | 6 pints separated milk.

20 lbs. potatoes.

HOME PRODUCE CONSUMED DURING THE WEEK.

2 lbs. jam. | 2 lbs. sprouts.

2 oz. onions.

MENU OF MEALS PROVIDED DURING THE WEEK.

	BREAKFAST.	DINNER.	TEA.
SUN. . . .	Tea, bread and butter, cold bacon.	Roast beef, suet dumplings, potatoes, sprouts, tea.	Tea, bread and butter, jam pastry, currant cakes.
MON. . .	Tea, bread and butter, porridge, bacon (for man).	Cold meat, bread and butter, pie, tea.	Tea, bread and butter, cake.
TUES. . .	Tea, bread and butter, porridge, bacon (for man).	Cold meat, potatoes, suet dumplings with currants.	Tea, bread and butter, pastry, bacon (man).
WED. . .	Tea, bread and butter, porridge, bacon (for man).	Hash, potatoes, pie.	Tea, bread and butter, pastry.
THUR. . .	Tea, bread and butter, porridge, bacon (for man).	Sausages, potatoes, dumplings with jam.	Tea, bread and butter, pastry, cold sausage (for man).
FRI. . . .	Tea, bread and butter, porridge, last scrap of bacon (for man).	Pork chops, potatoes, rice pudding, tea.	Tea, bread and butter, pastry.
SAT. . . .	Tea, bread and butter, pastry, porridge.	Boiled bacon, bread and butter, pastry, tea.	Tea, bread and butter, pastry, cakes.

This family takes no supper.

Study No. XXIX.—Leicestershire.

Man, wife, two sons, aged eleven and two, and one daughter, aged seven.

TOTAL WEEKLY EARNINGS OF FAMILY.

Wages—										*s.*	*d.*
Man	.	.	.	.	.	.	.	.	.	18	10
Son	.	.	.	.	.	.	.	.	.	0	9
										19	7

Extra earnings in the course of the year, £3 (30s. by the man, and 30s. by the woman).

Rent of cottage and garden, 1s. 10d. per week.

Rates, 12s. 6d. per year.

Mrs. Purcell is one of the finest types of country woman, bright and vigorous, and in a superlative degree " contriving." She likes the country, and would not live in a town if she had a chance.

" It's too much noise," she declares.

When she saw clearly the purpose of our inquiry, she gave all the help in her power. She opened her store cupboard, and showed us the array of pots of jam and crab-apple jelly and blackberry wine, all of which we were requested to sample. This year she has made about 8s. by sales of jam, and perhaps a couple of shillings by gathering and selling blackberries. One year she made seven and sixpence by gathering acorns—sold for the deer on the estate of a nobleman living near. In the shooting season they get a couple of rabbits given; moreover, there is a chance of buying dripping at 3d. a pound from " The Hall," of which the villagers are not slow to take advantage.

Some years ago she went out charing; but this has become impossible since the advent of her youngest child.

" Living is cheaper in the summer," she says. " In the summer I often manage with half a hundredweight of coal in the week. I let the fire go out through the day. But in the winter it takes me three hundredweight one week, and two another. This is a cold house."

Next door a brother lives whose wife is dead, and for whom she cleans up and washes. She gets no money for this, but he gives her garden produce from time to time, or she goes in and shares his meals when she has prepared them. At the time of the visit, however, this brother was working at a little distance, so that the number of persons sitting down to meals never varied.

Her husband earns 18s. 10d. weekly, of which he gives her 17s. The sum is exceptional; but his employer, when the Insurance Act became law, volunteered to pay the insurance for both, and also added 6d. to the wage. This was co-incident with their moving into a dearer cottage. They were formerly paying 1s. a week, and now the rent is about 1s. 10d. (£1, 5s. quarterly), so that financially their position is almost unchanged. But they have a larger garden, and though this year most of the potatoes have been bad, they have a good many greens, and can always, says Mrs. Purcell, beg a turnip. Then the garden contains rhubarb, from which she made part of her jam, and gooseberry bushes, and beets and cabbages to pickle. The vinegar bill for the year had amounted to 5s. She also makes mushroom ketchup, which, like the pickles, is chiefly used at home.

Two children are away from home, a boy and a girl—the one on a farm, the other in domestic service. Hitherto she has had no help from them, as they are earning but little. But she is doing all the mending and washing for the farm boy, who only lives three or four miles away, and visits her twice a week. He will pay her £1 when he gets his wage—paid yearly —at Martinmas. £1 is the regular estimate for a farm-hand's washing for the year. That pound she is resolved to set aside towards buying a pig; and as she has advanced the lad a little money for clothes, which he will repay when he settles his washing bill, doubtless the pig will be purchased.

The second boy, though only eleven, has been " earning " for twelve months, outside school hours. He goes to a butcher in the village before school, and again between morning and afternoon school, and when school is over. He generally gets a little breakfast—a bit of bread and a drink of tea—before starting, and a more substantial breakfast at the butcher's, as well as dinner and tea—though he often comes in for the fag-end of tea at home as well. On Saturdays he works the whole day, and brings home his week's wages—ninepence! It is rather heavy work for a child of eleven. He has, for instance, to carry heavy baskets of meat to a village a mile away, and his mother says " it bends him all sideways." But the ninepence is a welcome asset.

Mr. and Mrs. Purcell have been married eighteen years, and within that period Mrs. Purcell calculates that she has incurred and paid about £20 for doctors' bills. That includes £8 for confinements—she has had eight children, of whom five are living. One child had congestion of the lungs, and once they all had whooping-cough, whilst she herself was once very seriously ill. After all, a sum of £20 for doctors' bills for eighteen years is not abnormal. At present there is a trifling bill, incurred at Christmas, to be paid off, but nothing more.

Purcell is a steady, good fellow, who takes very little beer—perhaps sixpence worth in a week. Most of the meat is reserved for him.

" I love meat," says his wife, rather ruefully; " but I often go without. I've not touched it now for two days. I keep it for him; he *has* to have it."

Purcell's hours of work are long, beginning at 5 a.m. He gets back to tea about 6 p.m., but has to go once more at 8 p.m. to " bed the horses." He is a wagoner. Of course this means Sunday work—with more hours off, certainly, but three journeys, as on weekdays.

In the winter they use margarine, but in the summer they can generally buy " whey butter " at ninepence a pound from the neighbouring farmers. The tea is a high price, but Mrs. Purcell thinks it goes farther.

They sometimes buy golden syrup as a change from jam. Very occasionally Purcell's father makes them some small gift, such as sixpennyworth of fresh herrings. But for the most part they depend entirely on themselves.

The cottage, though rather cold and exposed, is a good one, with a pleasant living-room, a scullery, a pantry, a coal-shed, and two bedrooms.

The extra money earned by Mr. Purcell amounts to 30s. a year, for hay and harvest. Mrs. Purcell has the spending of it, and it is absorbed by all kinds of little expenses. For instance, on one occasion the father went over to see the daughter, who was in service, and on another they paid her fare home and back. Then sometimes a bill has been allowed to run to the extent of three or four shillings, or there are seeds to be purchased. Since their marriage they have bought no new blankets;

but a pair of sheets is needed every other year. As a rule they gather their wood, but they also spend about 3s. on it in the year. Again, they have just begun to pay rates—12s. 6d. annually.

It may be added that when the investigator descended upon Mrs. Purcell she was in some measure prepared. For three days running she had seen " a stranger on the grate "—a super-stition as popular in the country as in the town. So she resigned herself to the inevitable.

There is a deficiency of 13 per cent. of pro-tein in this family's dietary. Seven per cent. of the food consumed was payment in kind.

EXPENDITURE DURING TYPICAL WEEK IN JANUARY 1913.

	s.	d.		s.	d.
28 lbs. bread	3	2½	1 lb. candles	0	4
⅜ stone flour	0	8¼	Matches	0	1
1 lb. lard	0	7½	1 oz. tobacco	0	3½
1 lb. margarine . . .	0	6	Rent	1	10
4 lbs. sugar	0	8	½ lb. soap	0	1½
¼ lb. tea	0	7½	Mending cotton, laces .	0	2
6 oz. liver	0	2	Newspapers	0	3
4 fresh herrings . . .	0	3	Stamps	0	2
1 pint new milk, 2 pints			Insurance and State in-		
old milk	0	2½	surance	0	10
2 lbs. breast of mutton .	1	0	Man's pocket money. .	1	0
3¼ lbs. rump beef and			Shoes (weekly traveller)	1	0
⅛ lb. suet	2	1	Clothes do.	0	9
½ lb. currants . . .	0	2			
8 lbs. potatoes . . .	0	6		£1	0	0¼
2¼ cwt. coal	2	6			

3 lbs. cabbage. | 16 lbs. potatoes.

(Given by the brother for whom the woman manages.)

Menu of Meals provided during the Week.

	Breakfast.	Dinner.	Tea.
Sun. . . .	Tea, fresh herrings, bread and margarine.	Roast beef, potatoes, jam roly-poly.	Tea, bread and margarine or jam, currant cake.
Mon. . .	Tea, toast, dripping.	Bread and jam; man takes bread and cold meat with him.	Tea, cold meat and potatoes, cake.
Tues. . .	Tea, toast, dripping or lard.	Bread and jam; man takes bread and meat and cold tea with him.	Tea, tarts, cold meat, cabbage.
Wed. . .	Tea, toast, lard or margarine.	Bread and meat (woman), bread and jam (children); man takes bread and meat and cold tea with him.	Tea, cold meat, potatoes, tarts.
Thur. . .	Tea, toast, dripping, fried potatoes (man).	Bread and jam; man takes bread and meat with him.	Tea, fried liver, potatoes, jam roly-poly.
Fri. . . .	Tea, toast, lard, potatoes (for man).	Bread and jam, scrap of meat & bread (man).	Tea, roast mutton, potatoes, bread and jam.
Sat. . . .	Tea, toast, lard.	Bread and jam; man takes scrap of meat and bread with him.	Tea, mutton, potatoes, bread and margarine or jam.

The man and wife have a scrap of meat and bread and a drink of tea for supper on Sunday.

Study No. XXX.—East Riding of Yorkshire.

Man, wife, three sons, aged eight, six, and three, and two daughters, aged ten and five.

TOTAL WEEKLY EARNINGS OF FAMILY.

Wages—		s.	d.
Man		18	0
Wife		1	6½
		19	6½
Perquisites—			
Skimmed milk, say . .		0	7
	£1	0	1½

Extra earnings in the course of the year, £1, 16s.
Rent of cottage and garden, £5 per year.
Rates, 15s. per year.

The Atkinsons are pleasant, cordial country folk. Mrs. Atkinson is thin and worn, but unconquerably plucky, with the dash of humour that is like a glint of sunshine on the grim face of fortitude. Her husband, a stalwart man with very dark hair and a dark complexion —a contrast to his wife, who is fair and ruddy —seems to find it more difficult to see the humour of life and circumstances.

" A pound a week is t' least t' labourer can

do on," he says in broad Yorkshire. "*This*"
—his contemptuous accent indicated the weekly
wage—" don't hardlins run to mate. If ye get
a bit o' mate on t' Saturday, there's nowt on't
by t' Wednesday. An' everything's dear but
hard work. We addles more than we gets.
But I mun off ter t' thrashin'."

" Twenty-four's the least to my mind," says
Mrs. Atkinson when he is gone, " if you've
to feed *and* clothe 'em." She spoke as if the
latter process might conceivably be dispensed
with. " I know I've only five at home now,
and all little uns ; but if it wasn't for working
at the school, and for what my girls send me,
I'd be destitute."

Three girls are in service, and one is married,
while one boy is in farm-service, though he has
hitherto been too much of a rolling stone to
be able to help his mother. Just now the
married daughter is at home. She came for
her confinement, and the tiny grandchild, now a
month old, is sleeping in the cradle, so that
the two women are free to talk till the school
children come home. They are both shrewd
and intelligent, and the daughter is so quick

at mental arithmetic and ready of memory as to help considerably in the compilation of the household budget. But she is omitted from the calculations, since she is only a temporary visitor. She pays for whatever additional food she consumes, and the incomings and outgoings when she is absent are much more typical.

Mr. Atkinson earns 18s. weekly, and they have a quart of old milk allowed a day. His hours are from 6.30 a.m. to 6 p.m., with an hour for dinner. He also works on Sundays, going at 7 a.m. and again at 3 p.m. to " fodder t' cattle." For this Sunday work he was previously paid a shilling, which made the wage 19s. weekly. But the shilling has been docked since the Insurance Act came into operation, and his weekly fourpence is docked also. There is no extra money whatever, save at harvest-time, when he gets 27s. a week for four weeks, instead of 18s. The surplus money is generally " wared on shoes."

Mrs. Atkinson herself earns £4 yearly for the care of the schools. She has to provide all her own cleaning materials, to sweep and dust, to light fires in the winter, and to scrub the place out about five times a year. She also has to pay her weekly insurance of 3d. Some months ago she asked for " a rise; " but this audacious proposal is still under consideration, and will involve, doubtless, a number of solemn conclaves before it can even be entertained.

The rent is £5 yearly for a four-roomed cottage, with pretty good-sized rooms and a good garden, and the rates are 15s. They can always pick up sticks, and as they buy coals by the quarter of the ton, they are cheaper. For the last two or three weeks they have had a fire upstairs because one of the children was ill; but in the budget the normal winter expenditure on coal has been given.

This year potatoes have been " very bad indeed." As a rule, they last for six months in the year, from July to December inclusive, but this year they have only had a few basketfuls.

" How many potatoes do you use if you have plenty ? "

" We use half a stone at a meal."

That, of course, means unpeeled potatoes. For man and wife and five children it is not

an extravagant allowance. But at present they
are using cabbages at the rate of about 4 lbs.
to the meal. They would use them rather
more freely, but they want to make them " spin
out." It is not always easy to buy potatoes
in this village. Farmers object to breaking
into a " pie " for the sake of supplying mere
stones or half-stones, and generally they keep
by them only enough for their own consump-
tion.

There are onions in the garden, but only a
few.

" You don't keep a pig, do you ? "

" No ; what's the use of hungering ourselves
to feed a pig ? "

They seldom or never buy bacon. " Meat," the
mother and daughter both say, " is dearer than
in the nearest large town—7d. a pound for a
poor cut ! " We were shown the piece of meat
remaining over for Mr. Atkinson's dinner the
next day—after Sunday the meat is reserved
for the breadwinner. Speaking roughly, it was
$2\frac{1}{2}$ inches by 2 inches in surface, and $\frac{1}{4}$ inch
deep. Three-quarters of it was lean, the rest
was fat, or rather gristle, and it had a stringy,

depressing aspect. It might have weighed two ounces. But then this was " positively the last appearance " of the Sunday joint, which had previously appeared four times. Mrs. Atkinson always tries to keep some fragment back for her husband for the greater part of the week.

The daily quart of milk is a great help. It is skim milk, but one can always get another skim from it, and even secure a little cream for tea. And it means puddings, albeit they are only made with milk and water.

Of course here, as in other Yorkshire homes, " pie " or pastry is a great asset. Mrs. Atkinson makes about $2\frac{1}{4}$ stones of flour into bread and the rest into pie. We sampled one of these " pies." It was a huge, flat pasty, baked on one of the sheets of the oven—being nearly 2 feet long and $1\frac{1}{2}$ feet wide. It was substantial to the last degree, not too much lard having gone to the composition of the paste—Mrs. Atkinson generally uses $1\frac{1}{2}$ lbs. of lard in a week. Quite half an inch of this solid pastry was surmounted by a thin layer of " mince," and above was another crust, half as thick as the lower. But it was very palatable, and one can quite understand the value that is placed on these pies. They are supposed to contain a greater amount of support than mere bread and butter, and the Atkinsons contrive to keep them going all the week round. The " mince " was composed of currants, a little apple, and suet. More ordinarily, the pies are made with jam; but this inquiry belongs to January, and Christmas festivity is not yet wholly a thing of the past.

Mrs. Atkinson prefers country life, with all its limitations, to town life. There is a real home atmosphere in the cottage, though the village is a slow, sleepy place.

" Nothing happens in the year but one social."

There is a reading-room, for which the charge is 2d. weekly ; but there is nothing in the way of amusement for the young people. Still, they boast of the superiority of this village over the next, where there may or may not be more life, but certainly there is much more drinking.

It will be noted that rent is not included in the weekly expenditure. It is paid half-yearly, and Mrs. Atkinson looks to her own earnings, and perhaps help from her daughters, for its payment.

It may be said that the family is abnormally large, as there are ten children living. But it must be borne in mind that three at least of these are helping to support the home, while taking nothing from it; and that there is a sense in which, among the poor, children are regarded as an investment! We gathered that the girls in service probably contribute between them £4 yearly towards the home income. Thus the man's weekly wage is practically left free for current expenses.

The relation between this family and the farmer for whom they work seems to be quite pleasant. There is a possible grievance in the docking of the Sunday shilling; but very probably as regards this some rearrangement may yet be made later on. The pity is that, for the Atkinsons, with a lot so much easier than that of many labourers, life should still be, as they say, " only a putting on."

There is a deficiency of 12 per cent. of protein in this family's dietary, and of 2 per cent. of energy value. Eight per cent. of the food consumed is a perquisite, and about 2 per cent. is home produce.

EXPENDITURE DURING TYPICAL WEEK IN JANUARY 1913.

	s.	d.		s.	d.
3 stones flour . . .	5	6	1 cwt. coal	1	3
4 oz. yeast	0	3	1½ lbs. soap	0	4½
6 lbs. sugar	1	3	Man's club and insurance	0	8
1 lb. fresh butter . .	1	4	Woman's insurance . .	0	3
1 lb. Quaker oats . .	0	3	2 oz. tobacco . . .	0	7
1½ lbs. lard	1	0	*Christian Herald* . . .	0	1
½ lb. tea	0	10	Matches, blacking, black-		
1 lb. liver	0	4	lead, laces, etc. . .	0	2
5 lbs. beef (brisket) . .	2	11			
1½ lbs. rice (3d. per lb.				18	2½
in this village) . .	0	4½	Balance towards rates		
1 lb. currants . . .	0	4	and clothing . . .	1	4
1 cooking egg . . .	0	1			
3 pints oil	0	4½		19	6½

Nothing put away towards rent this week.

HOME PRODUCE CONSUMED DURING THE WEEK.
12 lbs. cabbage.

PERQUISITES CONSUMED DURING THE WEEK.
14 pints skimmed milk.

8

Menu of Meals provided during the Week.

	BREAKFAST.	DINNER.	TEA.	SUPPER.
SUN. .	Tea, bread and butter.	Beef, Yorkshire pudding, cabbage, tea.	Tea, toast, currant pastry.	Tea, pastry.
MON. .	Tea, bread and butter.	Cold meat, cabbage, tea.	Tea, toast, pastry.	Tea, bread and butter.
TUES. .	Tea, bread and butter.	Pudding made with Quaker oats, milk and water, bread, meat, and pastry (man).	Tea, bread and butter or fat.	Bread and butter or dripping from meat.
WED. .	Tea, bread and butter or dripping.	Cold meat (man), with bread and pastry, rice pudding, Quaker oats pudding, tea.	Tea, bread and butter or dripping, pastry.	Tea, bread and butter or dripping.
THUR. .	Tea, bread and scrape.	Liver, cabbages, pastry, bread.	Tea, bread and scrape, pastry.	Tea, bread or pastry.
FRI. .	Tea, bread and scrape.	Last scrap of meat (man), ricepudding pastry, tea.	Tea, bread and scrape, pastry.	Tea and " a bite of anything."
SAT. .	Tea, bread and scrape.	Any bread and fat or pastry that is left, tea.	Tea, any bread and fat or pastry that is left.	Tea, bread.

Only the man and woman have supper.

Study No. XXXI.—*Leicestershire.*

Man, wife, two sons, aged three and one, and five daughters, aged fourteen, eleven, seven, six, and four.

TOTAL WEEKLY EARNINGS OF FAMILY.

	s.	d.
Man's wage	18	0
Perquisites—		
Cottage and garden, say . . .	2	0
	20	0

Extra earnings in the course of the year, £1, 15s.

The Hopwoods are a large family. There are nine at home, the children's ages ranging from fourteen years to twelve months. But this does not exhaust the family; there are three " steps," Mr. Hopwood's children by a former marriage, who are out in the world, though occasionally the eldest son, a bricklayer, gets work on some contract in the neighbourhood. This enables him to lodge with his stepmother and augment her income.

" We live better if Tom's at home," says Mrs. Hopwood. " Then we get mutton sometimes for a change, though it's dearer ; and we get a bit of cheese."

The other stepchildren are girls, both in

domestic service. They cannot help financially to any extent, but they send all their cast-off clothing to be made up for the younger children, and for Bessie, the girl of fourteen, who will probably soon be out in service herself.

Mrs. Hopwood is a thoroughly well-meaning but not especially capable woman, and life weighs far too heavily upon her. But she has a patient, kindly face, and the two children under school age who are clinging to her gown are rosy and healthy, though Bessie looks somewhat anæmic.

There is not a great deal to cheer and encourage such a woman. The whole neighbourhood is decaying—so far as the labourer's prospects are concerned. There is nothing to keep the children on the land when they might be a stay to their parents. In this small village there is no reading-room, no young men's class, no mothers' meeting, "no anything!" There is no one to get up a good football or cricket club. The young fellows who remain in the village have nothing to do in the winter evenings but to "go to the public and play cards."

Of course financially the Hopwoods are better off than many people. They get 18s. a week, and a good-sized cottage free, with a garden. There is also some extra pay—15s. for " beer money," £1 at harvest, and a few shillings earned at haymaking at the rate of 3d. an hour, of which Mr. Hopwood has the spending, and the exact amount of which he alone knows. His harvest money generally has to provide his own clothes.

He works hard enough, being a wagoner. He is up at 5 a.m., back to breakfast between 7 and 7.30, when his wife cheers him with " dripping toast;" then away again with some bread and brawn in his pocket and a bottle of cocoa, and home to dinner at 3.30. Then there is work once more for an hour and a half, and another journey last thing in the evening to see that the horses are safe and comfortable for the night.

Three children go to school, and, since the school is a mile away, they take their lunch with them—bread and butter or bread and dripping. By the time that father has finished his dinner they are home and ready for tea, so that really from 3.30 to 5 seems to be one prolonged meal. But by 6 o'clock all the younger children are in bed. Mr. and Mrs. Hopwood, and sometimes the eldest girl, have a little supper, the remains of dinner, perhaps, or cocoa and toast, or possibly cake in the earlier part of the week.

Brawn can be bought in this village at 4d. per lb., and is said to be composed of pork and beef. At all events, the Hopwoods buy it instead of cheese or bacon, as it is so much cheaper. Her groceries are bought at an unusually cheap rate from some energetic tradesman who is trying to get the custom of the village. At present they are using potatoes very sparingly, and eating a good many swede turnips.

There is some debt weighing on Mrs. Hopwood's mind, though not a very great amount. She is quite clear with both her bakers, and to judge by the genial manner in which the grocer —who came round during the interview—addressed her, there can be no heavy debt in that quarter. Still, she owns to being behindhand. But now that one girl is fourteen and another eleven, she is hoping in the near future to have the burden lightened, and gradually to pay off all arrears.

In the budget given they have certainly outrun their income. On the other hand, the coal bill will be much reduced in summer, and Mr. Hopwood's beer money may wipe off a debt or two. Moreover, a little profit is made on the eldest son whenever he lodges with them.

Mrs. Hopwood has a sewing-machine, bought in the early years of her married life, with the help of which she makes almost all the children's clothes.

There is a deficiency of 29 per cent. of protein in this family's dietary, and of 19 per cent. of energy value. Four per cent. of the food consumed is home produce.

EXPENDITURE DURING TYPICAL WEEK IN JANUARY 1913.

	s.	d.		s.	d.
¼ stone flour	0	5½	4 lbs. flank of beef	2	0
1¼ lbs. self-raising flour	0	3	1½ lbs. best brisket and ¼ lb. suet	1	0
1 lb. best margarine	1	0	⅓ lb. rice	0	0¾
1 lb. dripping	0	6	2½ stones turnips	0	2
¾ lb. currants	0	3	1 lb. candles	0	3
44 lbs. bread	5	0½	1 quart oil	0	3
3½ pints new milk	0	5¼	Coal	1	8
6 lbs. sugar	0	10½	Matches, laces, thread, soap	0	2
1 lb. golden syrup	0	3	Man's pocket money (including insurance, club)	1	0
¼ lb. tea	0	4½	Children's insurance	0	3
¼ lb. cocoa	0	4½			
½ lb. bacon	0	5			
½ lb. black pudding	0	2			
3 lbs. brawn	1	0			
1½ pints old milk	0	1½			
4 fresh herrings	0	3		18	7

HOME PRODUCE CONSUMED DURING THE WEEK.

8½ lbs. potatoes.	5 lbs. parsnips.
½ lb. carrots.	1½ lbs. onions.

MENU OF MEALS PROVIDED DURING THE WEEK.

	BREAKFAST.	DINNER.	TEA.	SUPPER.
SUN. .	Black pudding, bacon, bread, tea.	Roast beef, potatoes and turnips, suet pudding with currants.	Tea, bread and butter, cake.	Meat, remaining vegetables, or bread and treacle, cocoa.
MON. .	Bread and margarine or dripping, tea.	Bacon, bread and cocoa (for man), bread and dripping (for school children); the rest have bread and margarine or treacle.	Tea, cold meat, potatoes, turnips, bread pudding.	Toast or cake, cocoa.
TUES.	Bread and margarine, tea.	Brawn, bread and cocoa (for man), bread and margarine for all the others.	Tea, hashed meat with onions, turnips, bread, pastry.	Bread and scraps of meat or brawn, cocoa.
WED. .	Bread and margarine or treacle, tea.	Same as on Tuesday.	Tea, hash with onions, potatoes (for man), swedes, rice pudding.	Bread and margarine or brawn, cocoa.
THUR.	Bread and margarine or dripping, tea.	Same as on Tuesday.	Tea, roast meat, potatoes, turnips, boiled suet pudding with currants, bread.	Bread and scraps of meat, cocoa.
FRI. .	Bread and margarine or dripping toast, tea.	Same as on Tuesday.	Tea, cold meat, potatoes, swedes, bread and margarine.	Bread and margarine, tea.
SAT. .	Bread and margarine or dripping, tea.	Same as on Tuesday.	Tea, hash with onions, parsnips, and carrots, fresh herrings, bread.	Remaining fresh herrings, bread, cocoa.

The baby has a little bread and milk. The children take bread and margarine or dripping with them to school for dinner.

Study No. XXXII.—Leicestershire.

Man, wife, two sons, aged five and three.

TOTAL WEEKLY EARNINGS OF FAMILY.

	s.	d.
Man's wage	18	0
Perquisites—		
Cottage and garden, say	2	0
	20	0

Extra earnings in the course of the year, £1.

The Kays are a good-looking couple, still on the sunny side of thirty. They occupy a really superior cottage with a spacious living-room, small scullery, pantry, short passage, and two bedrooms, one as large as the living-room, the other occupying the space above scullery, pantry, and passage. There is a good garden, and also an allotment, which goes with the house, so that they generally have vegetables of one kind or another all the year round. At present, however, they are using potatoes very sparingly, at the rate often of a pound and a half to a meal, hoping to make them hold out till new ones come in. They are fortunate in having an apple tree, and gooseberries and currants, out of which Mrs. Kay, when the season is good, makes a quantity of jam for home use. Just now she is using it at the rate of a 2-lb. jar a week. They do not regard the garden as a means of making money, for if they earn a few shillings by selling the produce in a good year, they have to buy in a bad one, while the land takes a certain amount of upkeep, with seeds, manure, etc. It is true that as they keep a pig most of the year they have to buy only one load of manure at 5s.

Mr. Kay gets 18s. a week and his cottage. The only additional money is £1 at Michaelmas. But his work is quite regular. It is generally harder in winter than in summer, when the cows are turned out to grass ; and it is in summer that he cultivates his own garden, his wife helping him, before the press of harvest comes on and he has to work late for his employer.

The hours at present (January) are about 5.30 a.m. to 6 p.m., and on Sundays 5.30 a.m. to 10.30 a.m. and from 3.30 to 6. But it may be conjectured that hard work suits him, since he is a fresh-complexioned young fellow, with an open, pleasant face.

They keep a pig nine months of the year, saving up to buy it in the other three months. They do not sell any of it, and what with pork and bacon it lasts them the whole year round. For the last pig they paid 28s., and Mrs. Kay calculated roughly that its food must have cost nearly £4. Still, it rather more than paid its expenses; they are still consuming bacon at the rate of 2 lbs. a week, and are setting aside all the while potato-parings for " swill," which we hope will not be in too advanced a state of decomposition before the next pig arrives to sample it.

Altogether, in spite of hard work, these people live a gray but not unhappy life. Mrs. Kay knits all the socks, and washes, makes, and mends with great skill and energy. The extra £1 at Michaelmas is largely absorbed by Mr. Kay's winter shoes; what is over goes towards shoes for the boys. The clothing club is a help; but when an extra pair of shoes, or any other item of clothing, has to be bought, much contrivance is necessary in order to pay ready money. They do not actually dock the food to any extent, but the baker probably has to take his money by instalments for two or three weeks.

The amount of oil used is rather large, but they keep a lamp burning in the passage. This, like the two newspapers, might be entered under the heading of "luxuries."

There is a deficiency of 13 per cent. of protein in this family's dietary. One-tenth of the food consumed is home produce.

EXPENDITURE DURING TYPICAL WEEK IN JANUARY 1913.

	s.	d.		s.	d.
6 lbs. sugar	1	·0	Clothing club . . .	0	6
½ lb. butter	0	7½	Towards purchase of pig	1	0
6 oz. tea	0	6	Coal and wood . . .	1	9
7 pints new milk . . .	0	10½	2½ quarts oil, matches,		
¼ lb. currants . . .	0	1	candles	0	9
4½ lbs. beef (shoulder) and			Blacklead, blacking, bath-		
¼ lb. suet	3	0	brick, laces, etc. . .	0	1½
1½ oz. cocoa	0	1½	Insurance	0	4
½ lb. lard	0	3½	Club	0	5
¼ lb. golden syrup . .	0	1½	Wool, cotton	0	2
20 lbs. bread	2	6	Newspapers	0	3
Baking powder . . .	0	2	Collections	0	1
5¼ lbs. flour	0	9	Oranges	0	1
1 lb. liver	0	4			
½ lb. Quaker oats . .	0	1½		17	0
Custard powder, salt,					
pepper, ginger, vinegar	0	1½	Balance towards boots		
¼ lb. rice	0	0½	and clothes . . .	1	0
2 oz. tobacco	0	7			
1 lb. soap, blue, starch .	0	3½		18	0

HOME PRODUCE CONSUMED DURING THE WEEK.

2 lbs. bacon.	3 lbs. sprouts.
9 lbs. potatoes.	2 lbs. apples.

4 oz. onions.

Menu of Meals provided during the Week.

	Breakfast.	Dinner.	Tea.
Sun. . . .	Tea, bacon and bread.	Roast beef, greens and potatoes, suet pudding with apples.	Tea, bread and butter, ginger-cake.
Mon. . . .	Tea, bacon and bread.	Cold beef, potatoes, jam pastry, milk pudding (rice).	Tea, bread and butter or dripping toast, cake.
Tues.. . .	Tea, bacon and bread, porridge for children.	Cold meat, potatoes, sprouts, suet pudding with currants, cocoa.	Tea, bread and butter or dripping toast, cake.
Wed.. . .	Tea, bacon and bread.	Hashed meat with onion, potatoes, boiled jam pudding.	Tea, bread and butter or jam or treacle.
Thur. . .	Tea, bacon and bread, porridge for children.	Fried liver with onion, potatoes, boiled dripping pudding, rice pudding.	Tea, bread and butter or jam.
Fri. . . .	Tea, bacon and bread.	Fried meat with onion, potatoes, sprouts, boiled pudding with treacle.	Tea, bread and jam or butter.
Sat. . . .	Tea, bacon and bread, porridge for children.	Bread and butter, rice pudding, cocoa.	Tea, bread and jam.

Tea is sometimes drunk at dinner-time, sometimes cocoa, and sometimes neither. Supper is only taken on Sundays, and consists of bread and butter, or cake, and cocoa.

Study No. XXXIII.—Essex.

Man, wife; five sons, aged fifteen, nine, seven, five, and three; and one daughter, aged fourteen.

TOTAL WEEKLY EARNINGS OF FAMILY.

	s.	d.
Wages—		
Man	15	0
Son	3	0
	18	0
Perquisites—		
Cottage and garden, say	2	0
	20	0

Extra earnings in the course of the year, £2, 4s. (man, £1, 4s.; woman, £1).

Atkinson is a horseman under a very good master, and receives a free cottage, 15s. a week, and about 24s. extra at harvest-time. The eldest boy has just begun to earn 3s. a week and his dinner. The woman earns £1 a year at pea-picking. By an ancient right the family is entitled to a certain amount of free wood, which the farmer leads for them.

The cottage is one of a pair, with a very large downstairs room and three bedrooms. The

garden, of about one-eighth of an acre, is awk-
wardly shaped and overhung with trees. When
we called at noon the woman looked rather
untidy, and so did the living-room. The win-
dow, however, had clean white curtains, and
was adorned with a few plants. The furniture
was rough but fairly substantial, and two or
three imposing pots and pans occupied the
kitchen range. A strong, healthy child of three
was toddling about.

The woman was London born, but as a girl
she went into the country to be with her grandmother, and her next step was to enter service
at a farmhouse at £10 a year. There she laid
by a few pounds. Her future husband, a born
agricultural labourer, sober and steady, was
working on the same farm, and finally they
married. With their joint savings they bought
the furniture and a pretty good supply of bed-
ding. They have practically spent nothing
since on either of these items. Mrs. Atkinson
was evidently thrifty and industrious and a
good needlewoman, making all her children's
clothes herself.

Their daily dinner consists of potatoes and

suet dumplings, and on Sunday they have gravy and meat. They eat cheese and butter, but no bacon and no eggs, and the wife complained that they would be very badly off but for the garden. With their bread they have dripping, butter, or jam—this week only the two former. She said that though they never felt actually hungry after their dinner, they were never " completely satisfied like," except on Sundays.

The family has, apparently, run slightly into debt in anticipation of the pea-picking and harvest money, although this has to provide the funds for clothing, or possibly doctor's bills.

If Atkinson lost his situation and had to accept a lower wage, the first economy would be on the groceries. His wife declared emphatically that the country is far dearer to live in than London. They buy all their stores from travelling carts, the town being three miles distant.

The family recently removed from a two-roomed cottage, where the eldest boy used to sleep on a couch in the living-room, and they thought that the children had been decidedly stronger for it. They are all pretty healthy, and never suffer from anything but " colds on the chest," for which she rubs them with camphorated oil. The only luxury they seem to indulge in is a weekly newspaper.

There is a deficiency of 12 per cent. of protein in this family's dietary. One-twelfth of the food consumed is home produce.

EXPENDITURE DURING TYPICAL WEEK IN OCTOBER 1912.

	s.	d.		s.	d.
5 lbs. sugar	0	11½	2 lbs. bones	0	2
46 lbs. bread	5	9	1 cwt. coal	1	4
7½ oz. tea	0	9½	1 lb. soap	0	3
1¼ lbs. butter	1	3	½ gallon oil	0	4½
1 lb. cheese	0	8½	Laces, cotton, household		
1 lb. rice	0	2	sundries	0	2
1 lb. Quaker oats	0	3			
2 lbs. flank beef	1	2		16	8
½ lb. suet	0	4	Towards clothing and re-		
16 lbs. flour	2	0	payment of debt	1	4
3 pints milk	0	4½			
¼ lb. lard	0	2		18	0
½ lb. pork	0	3½			
¼ lb. chocolate powder	0	2			

HOME PRODUCE CONSUMED DURING THE WEEK.

7 lbs. cabbage.	4 lbs. carrots.
22 lbs. potatoes.	1 lb. beetroot.

GIFTS CONSUMED DURING THE WEEK.
6 lbs. apples.

MENU OF MEALS PROVIDED DURING THE WEEK.

	BREAKFAST.	DINNER.	TEA.	SUPPER.
SUN. . .	Bread and butter, tea.	Suet pudding, meat, savoys.	Bread and butter, tea.	None.
MON. .	Bread and butter, tea.	Suet pudding, meat, vegetables.	Bread and butter, tea.	Bread and cheese.
TUES. .	Bread and butter, bread and sugar, tea.	Potatoes, apple pudding, rice.	Bread and butter, tea.	Bread and butter.
WED. .	Bread and butter, tea, porridge.	Suet dumplings, potatoes, carrots.	Bread and butter, bread pudding, tea.	Bread and cheese.
THUR. .	Bread and butter, tea.	Dripping, potatoes, carrots, pork.	Bread and butter, apple pie, tea.	None.
FRI. . .	Bread, toast, pork, tea.	Soup, potatoes, bread.	Bread and butter, tea.	Bread and cheese.
SAT. . .	Bread and butter, tea, cocoa.	Dumpling, soup, potatoes, savoys.	Bread and sugar, tea.	Bread and beetroot.

Only one person in this family takes supper.

A little tea or cocoa and bread and cheese is eaten between the 5.30 breakfast and dinner.

Study No. XXXIV.—Berkshire.

Man, wife; four sons, aged fourteen, nine, six, and two; and five daughters, aged twelve, eleven, seven, four, and four months.

TOTAL WEEKLY EARNINGS OF FAMILY.

Wages—	*s.*	*d.*
Man	13	0
Son	6	0
	19	0
Perquisites—		
Cottage and garden, say . .	2	0
	21	0

Extra earnings in the course of the year, £3, 15s.

Mrs. Warren is a very reserved, scrupulously clean woman, of a type often called superior. Probably she will never be frank enough about her troubles to get much help from the charitably disposed; and her husband, if possible, is more reserved than she is. These people would have given no help if we had not convinced them that their experience might indirectly be of use to other people. But once convinced, they helped right willingly ; for they were intelligent enough to see that all reform must be based on first-hand knowledge of facts.

How they *have* lived is still a mystery, for now there is a boy earning 6s. a week. He is only fourteen, but he left school at the age of thirteen. The eldest child is a girl of fifteen, and she has gone into service and is practically off her parents' hands. Even so, there are eleven at home in the four-roomed cottage, the children's ages ranging from fourteen years to four months. They are fairly healthy as a rule, though next week Dorothy, the child of seven, will have to go to the eye hospital.

Mr. Warren gets 13s. a week, with the house. He starts work at 5 a.m.—he is a carter—and comes home to breakfast a little after 6. He is back at work at 7, taking a slice of bread and cheese with him, and goes on till 3, when he has an hour for dinner. At present he gets back finally at about 5.45 p.m. The boy works with his father, and has the same hours. He is really worth more than 6s. a week ; but, as his mother says rather wistfully, " he is not very old."

There is some Sunday work, but only about three hours.

We asked their opinion on the matter of debts incurred by labourers with young families, and Mrs. Warren spoke out of her own hard experience, as it afterwards transpired. She thought that debts could very seldom amount to £15, or even £10.

" One shop tells another—I've heard them doing it—about other people. They tell us such as we *must* pay ready money, for if we can't pay this week, it isn't likely we can pay next."

She thought a debt of £2 or £3 to one tradesman was possible, but not more, unless conditions were quite unusual. She said, too, that " the shops were worse than they used to be " in this matter of giving credit. This seems likely to be true, as facilities for leaving the village are greater than they once were. Mrs. Warren herself is heavily in arrears at a village some miles distant.

She manages to get a piece of meat for the two breadwinners every day, or nearly every day. Like many another, she apportions out the meat at the beginning of the week, and keeps back so much " to look at." It is said in this neighbourhood of the women and children, " they eat the potatoes and look at the meat." Frequently they only cook part of the joint on Sundays ; but anyhow it has to last the week in a really " managing " household— unless, as in the budget now given, a smaller joint is bought than the wage allows and something is spent on bacon. In this out-of-the-way village it is difficult to get fish or liver, or the famous and popular dainty known as " pig's pluck." Any such shopping must be done four miles away.

" But of course there is extra money ? "

" Yes. This Michaelmas we had 50s. I don't know what we shall get next spring ; we haven't been here long enough ; but once he earned 25s. extra going with the binder. It's then we try to pay off all that has got behind. I do my best to put 1s. by one week for clothes and another week for shoes ; but now that we're using more coal and oil it's almost impossible. We go to a second-hand shop sometimes ; we got a coat and waistcoat for Harry that way

for 8s., and my husband paid 6s. for a jacket
and 8s. for trousers. But the shoes—I can
never get straight with the shoes ! "

It must be remembered that this woman has
also to buy more dress material, calico and the
like, for the children than women who get more
" cast-offs " given.

The meat bill is sometimes reduced to 1s. ;
but on the whole the week given may be regarded as typical.

There is a deficiency of 35 per cent. of protein
in this family's dietary, and of 22 per cent. of
energy value. One-tenth of the food consumed
is home produce.

EXPENDITURE DURING TYPICAL WEEK IN NOVEMBER 1912.

	s.	d.		s.	d.
56 lbs. bread	6	5	2½ cwt. coal and wood .	3	3
½ stone flour	0	11	Insurance and club . .	0	7
4 lbs. sugar	0	8	1 quart oil, candles, and		
2½ pints milk	0	3½	matches	0	4½
½ lb. tea	0	8	Soap, soda, etc. . . .	0	1½
2 lbs. oatmeal . . .	0	4			
1 lb. lard	0	10		18	0
½ lb. butter	0	6½	Balance put by for clothes		
½ lb. cheese	0	4½	and shoes, etc. . .	1	0
1 lb. bacon	0	8			
2 lbs. golden syrup . .	0	5½		19	0
1 lb. rice	0	2			
4 lbs. frozen meat and ½					
lb. suet	1	4			

Home Produce consumed during the Week.

35 lbs. potatoes. | 5 lbs. parsnips.
1 lb. onions.

Menu of Meals provided during the Week.

	BREAKFAST.	DINNER.	TEA.
SUN. . . .	Bread and butter, tea.	Roast meat, suet pudding, potatoes, parsnips.	Tea, bread and lard or golden syrup.
MON. . . .	Porridge, bread and butter, tea.	Cold meat (for man and son), bread, potatoes, tea.	Tea, bread and lard or golden syrup.
TUES. . .	Porridge, bread and butter, tea.	Stewed meat, dumplings, onions, potatoes.	Tea, bread and butter or golden syrup.
WED. . . .	Porridge, bread and butter, tea.	Boiled bacon, suet pudding.	Tea, bread and butter or golden syrup.
THUR. . .	Porridge, bread and lard, tea.	Cold bacon, rice, potatoes, tea.	Tea, bread and lard.
FRI. . . .	Porridge, bread and lard, tea.	Bacon, rice, dumplings.	Tea, bread and lard, or butter or golden syrup.
SAT. . . .	Porridge, bread (sugar sprinkled on bread), tea.	Bread and butter, tea.	Tea, bread and lard.

No supper. The man and son take a little bread and cheese with them to eat between breakfast and dinner.

Man, wife, two sons, aged four and two, and one niece, aged ten.

TOTAL WEEKLY EARNINGS OF FAMILY.

Wages—

		s.	d.
Man	.	18	0
Wife	.	1	6
		19	6

Perquisite—

Cottage and small garden, say	2	0
	21	6

No extra earnings.

Mrs. Walker is a delicate-looking woman of about eight-and-twenty. Her life is a constant struggle, but this is partly due to untoward circumstances. For one thing, her husband's father, for whom he worked, failed some years ago, and on beginning life afresh claimed for his own use the furniture which he had given to his son on the latter's marriage. This meant that the younger Walkers had to buy fresh furniture on the instalment system, for which they are still paying at the rate of 1s. 6d. a week.

Another eighteen months must pass before the debt is paid off.

Again, there has been a doctor's bill of £3, 17s., which they are gradually diminishing at the rate of 3s. a month. It covers Mrs. Walker's last confinement and a number of visits paid last year when the children had bronchitis.

Walker earns 18s. weekly and his cottage. It is three-roomed—one good living-room, which has to be pantry and scullery too, and two bedrooms. The garden is very small. It is not large enough to grow potatoes, but they get some peas, beans, and sprouts. At present, however, the supply is quite exhausted.

There is no harvest money and no hay money. Sometimes Walker has worked from 3 in the morning to 10.45 p.m., without so much as a free breakfast; that meal has been taken to him by his wife at 6 a.m. But his general hours are from 6 a.m. to 6 p.m. On Sundays, at present, he is working from 6 to 10.30 a.m. and from 3.30 to 6 p.m.

Mrs. Walker herself goes once or twice a week to help her mother, who takes in washing. She finds her own food, but earns, on an average, 1s. 6d. a week.

They have two little boys of their own, aged two and four; but they have also taken complete charge of Mrs. Walker's orphaned niece, a little girl nearly ten years old. And, curiously enough, they do not regard this additional burden as a burden at all, but as a source of happiness.

Walker takes his lunch with him, as he has a twenty minutes' walk to his work. This means late dinner, a little after 6 p.m.

They are not extravagant, save in the matter of coals, which in the winter they use at the rate of three hundredweight a week. Sticks are picked up and brought home by the husband. They pay 1s. 10d. a week altogether for insurance, including State insurance. The boys and Mrs. Walker's mother are also insured, and Walker is in a sick club. The children's insurance secures them £5 each when they leave school and start work; the mother's insurance is on her death.

Clothes are bought mainly on the instalment system, and they pay 1s. a week regularly to a traveller. Any additional outlay means short-age in the food. The man's shoes cost 8s. 6d. a pair, and only last about six months.

He does not breakfast before going to work, but takes bread and butter and tea and sugar with him, and is allowed boiling water. No milk at all is consumed in this household ex-cept on Sundays, when Mrs. Walker's father gets a quart of old milk given, and gives his daughter half. Thus on Sundays they have a small rice pudding in addition to roly-poly. This week they have been using jam; sometimes golden syrup takes its place, but never by any chance are both purchased in one week.

Mrs. Walker is not discontented, on the whole, though the doctor's bill and the perpetual pay-ing out for the furniture are rather depressing circumstances. But she ekes out the family income with her own 1s. 6d., and hopes, when her niece is a little older and the younger children are off to school, to secure some addi-tional washing or charing, and earn consider-ably more.

At Christmas they get a 7-lb. joint of beef, given by some local magnate.

There is a deficiency of 36 per cent. of protein in this family's dietary, and of 30 per cent. of energy value. One per cent. of the food consumed is given by the woman's father.

EXPENDITURE DURING TYPICAL WEEK IN JANUARY 1913.

	s.	d.		s.	d.
2 lbs. sugar	0	4	1 lb. jam	0	3½
¼ lb. tea	0	4½	3 cwt. coal	2	9
½ lb. lard	0	3½	2 quarts oil and 1 lb. candles	0	8½
½ lb. butter	0	7½			
½ lb. cheese	0	4½	1 lb. soap	0	3
½ lb. pork sausages	0	4	Towards clothing	1	0
8 lbs. potatoes	0	4	1 oz. tobacco	0	3½
3¼ lbs. steak and ¼ lb. suet	2	0	Instalment on furniture	1	6
½ stone flour	1	0	State insurance, sick clubs (children and mother)	1	10
18 lbs. bread	2	3			
1 lb. bacon	0	10			
¼ lb. rice	0	0½		18	8
2 pints beer	0	6	Balance towards doctor's bill	0	10
1 lb. liver	0	4			
½ lb. brawn	0	3		19	6
¼ lb. currants	0	1			
1 lb. onions	0	1			

GIFT CONSUMED DURING THE WEEK.
1 pint old milk.

MENU OF MEALS PROVIDED DURING THE WEEK.

	BREAKFAST.	DINNER.	TEA.
SUN. . . .	Tea with sugar but no milk, bread and sausages.	Roast meat, potatoes, rice pudding, jam roly-poly.	Tea (without milk), bread and butter, currant cake.
MON. . .	Tea, bread and bacon, bread and butter.	Bread and cheese (man), bread and butter (for the others).	Cold meat, potatoes, roly-poly pudding.
TUES. . .	Tea, bread and bacon, bread and butter.	Bread and cheese (man), bread and butter (for the others).	Hash, with potatoes and onions, bread and butter.
WED. . .	Tea, bread and bacon, bread and butter.	Bread and cheese (man), bread and bacon (for the others).	Tea, fried liver with onions and potatoes, bread.
THUR. . .	Tea, bread and bacon, bread and butter.	Bread and cheese (man), bread and butter for the others.	Tea, hashed meat with onions and potatoes, currant dumpling, bread and butter or jam.
FRI. . . .	Tea, bread and bacon, bread and butter.	Bread and cheese (man), bread and butter (for the others).	Tea, remainder of liver fried with onions and potatoes.
SAT. . . .	Tea, bread and bacon, bread and butter.	Bread and cheese (man), bread and jam or butter (for the others).	Tea, bacon, bread and butter.

The man and woman have bread and cheese and beer for supper on Saturday and Sunday. Only the woman and children have bacon for breakfast.

Study No. XXXVI.—North Riding of Yorkshire.

Man, wife, two sons, aged fourteen and four, and one daughter, aged eleven.

TOTAL WEEKLY EARNINGS OF FAMILY.

	s.	d.
Wages—		
Man	17	0
Wife	5	0
	22	0

Rent of cottage, £4 per year.
Rent of allotment, 12s. per year.
No extra earnings.

Mrs. Bob Wilson is a thoroughly capable woman, who does her best to supplement her husband's earnings by her own. She has not always been able to do this, as illness and the care of her younger boy hampered her; but last April she bought a wringer on the instalment system, and since then she believes that she has, for the most part, averaged 5s. a week. On one occasion, but only one, she made 8s.; but over a number of weeks we found 5s. the average. This represents regular work—from Tuesday morning to Thursday afternoon. The work is done at home.

Last Martinmas there came in an additional sum of £1, from a farm hand for whom she had washed for a year. Ten shillings of it went in shoes for the children, and ten towards a doctor's bill. She does not expect anything extra next Martinmas, as the young fellow who employed her has left the village.

There are three children—Jack, nearly fourteen; Jessie, a delicate girl of eleven; and a child of four. The first two are Mr. Wilson's children by a previous marriage. The girl has cost them a good deal in cod-liver oil and the like.

Wilson regularly gives his wife 14s. out of his 17s. a week. Out of the other 3s. he pays the rent of the house (£4 yearly), and that of the allotment (12s. yearly), or the bulk of these. He also buys his own tobacco, and pays his insurance. He gets no overtime or Michaelmas money, and no perquisites.

In the winter he starts work at 7 a.m., taking his dinner with him, and leaves at 5 p.m. In the summer the hours are from 6.30 a.m. to 5.30 p.m. On Mondays it is 8 p.m., as he helps in the laundry of the institution for which he works; and though he gets no extra money for this overtime, he has tea provided. The rest of the week he works on the land.

Last year they sold 40 stones of potatoes, which probably helped to buy clothing. This year they will not be able to sell a single stone. They only got four sacks out of their ground, and there are two left, which they are using carefully, at the rate of 4 lbs. a day. They could do with nearly twice as many, as they are all fond of potatoes.

A shilling every week goes towards paying off the cost of the wringer, which was 37s. They owe the doctor £2, 12s. 6d.; but he knows the family well, and " doesn't mind if he gets it at 6d. a week."

Since Mrs. Wilson began to earn money pretty regularly, she has actually bought herself " a long coat and a blouse." The price of the coat was 18s. Then the older boy has had a suit, costing 19s. 11d., which will last him a full year. These things are generally paid for at the rate of 2s. 6d. a fortnight. They are bought from " the men who come round."

9

Mrs. Wilson has a sister living not far away, who, though not well off, is a clever dressmaker, and helps her by making clothing for Jessie, who sometimes also gets the clothes outgrown by a cousin.

They keep poultry, but hitherto have hardly realized anything by them. Early in the year they sold some pullets at 1s. 4d. each, partly because their food was so expensive—2s. weekly. At present they have fourteen fowls, and as Mrs. Wilson is earning more, and can afford to feed them, these will soon probably pay very well; meanwhile, though, they use two or three eggs a week themselves.

The wood is gathered by the elder boy. Mrs. Wilson gets her household utensils, table-cloths, etc., from a tea company, which sells tea at a high price, but also gives coupons exchangeable for " almost anything." The dripping is bought at a very cheap rate from the institution where Wilson works.

It will be obvious that but for Mrs. Wilson's earnings these people would hardly be able to pay their way.

As it is, their dietary shows a deficiency of

22 per cent. of protein and of 2 per cent. of energy value. One-twelfth of the food consumed is home produce.

EXPENDITURE DURING TYPICAL WEEK IN DECEMBER 1912.

	s.	d.		s.	d.
2 stones flour . . .	3	6	½ lb. cheese	0	4½
Yeast	0	1	Salt, blacking, hearth-		
1 lb. butter	1	4	stone, cotton, etc. .	0	2
1½ lbs. lard	1	0	2 lbs. dripping . . .	0	6
2 lbs. bacon	1	8	Corn and meal for		
½ lb. currants . . .	0	2½	poultry	1	0
2 lbs. sugar	0	5	Payment towards		
6 pints milk . . .	0	8	mangle	1	0
½ lb. tea with trading			Payment Clothing club.	1	3
premium	1	3			
¼ lb. baking powder .	0	2½		19	3
1 quart oil	0	3	Balance kept by man		
½ lb. candles	0	2½	for rent, rates, clothes,		
2 lbs. pie beef, 2 oz.			tobacco, insurance,		
suet	1	1	club	3	0
4 bloaters	0	3			
2 cwt. coal	2	6	£1	2	3
Soap, soda	0	4			

HOME PRODUCE CONSUMED DURING THE WEEK.

16 lbs. potatoes.	1½ lbs. onions.
8 lbs. swedes.	2 eggs.

MENU OF MEALS PROVIDED DURING THE WEEK.

	BREAKFAST.	DINNER.	TEA.	SUPPER.
SUN. .	Fried bacon, bread, tea.	Meat pie, Yorkshire pudding, potatoes, swedes.	Tea, bread and butter, cakes (home made).	A little of the meat from dinner, cake.
MON. .	Bread and butter, tea.	Bread and butter, pastry, tea.	Tea, bread and butter, pastry.	Tea, bread and butter.
TUES. .	Bread and butter, tea.	Bread and butter, pastry, tea.	Tea, stew, potatoes and onions.	None.
WED. .	Bread and butter or dripping, tea.	Bread and butter or dripping, pastry, tea.	Tea, onions and potatoes cooked with dripping, and swedes.	Tea, bread and cheese.
THUR. .	Bread and butter or dripping, tea.	Bread and butter, pastry, tea.	Tea, bloaters, bread and butter, pastry.	None.
FRI. .	Bread and dripping, tea.	Bread and butter, tea.	Tea, potatoes, onions, suet dumplings, bread and butter.	Tea, pastry or bread.
SAT. .	Bread and butter, tea.	Bread and dripping, pastry, tea.	Tea, bread and butter or pastry.	Tea, fried bacon, bread.

The children have supper only on Sundays.

Wilson takes bacon or cheese with bread and pastry with him for dinner.

Study No. XXXVII.—Oxfordshire.

Man, wife, four sons aged sixteen, thirteen, nine, and three, and one daughter aged ten.

TOTAL WEEKLY EARNINGS OF FAMILY.

Wages—	s.	d.
Man	13	6
Wife	1	6
Son	8	0
	23	0

Extra earnings in course of the year, £3, 16s.
Rent of cottage, £4, 5s.
Rent of allotment, 14s.

The Richard Abbotts are looked upon by the village generally as being " out of the wood," because the eldest boy is earning 8s. a week. He gives his mother 6s., and the remainder covers insurance and clothes. One girl of fifteen is now away from home, but not earning enough to help those left behind.

They are certainly a great deal better off than they were ; but they still have to count every penny. The rent of the four-roomed house is £4, 5s., paid yearly, and their allotment is 3s. 6d. per quarter. That allotment is partly covered with corn, which this year was sold for the substantial sum of 16s. 6d., and helped to pay the house rent. It also provided some pickings (called " tail-corns " by Mrs. Abbott) for the poultry. She keeps poultry, and calculates that, if in luck, she makes £2 clear profit by them in the year. But last year she was unlucky. She spends 6d. a week on their corn.

" How much does your husband get with piece-work and overtime ? " we asked. She answered promptly,—

" Hoeing and harvest together came to £3, 6s. this year. That was good; it depends a great deal on the weather. The haymaking extra money — that wasn't more than 10s. Then— I forgot to tell you—for the five winter months that he does Sunday work, about five or six hours every Sunday, he gets 1s. 6d. a week. Then I get 1s. a week for looking after the house next door ; and sometimes, once a month, or once a fortnight, as it happens, I go out for a day and earn 1s. 6d. So you may count my earnings at 1s. 6d. a week—that's all it comes to."

" Still, you're well off compared with many."

" Oh, that we are ! But, if you'll believe me, I've never begun to pay off my debts yet. I shall begin, all well, when John is fourteen. I'm keeping straight at the shops now, of course, but somehow I can't put any by, not to give the children what's right. You see, there's seven at home. And this is a big room—we use a hundred and a quarter of coal in the winter."

" Do you have to buy wood ? "

" We pick it up when we can, if we get leave of the farmer ; but one can't be always asking leave. I've been buying it since last March— five faggots for 1s. ; they last three weeks or a month."

" How about the clothing ? "

" Well, my sister, living farther south, sends me all the old things she can. But she's none too well off, and she can't give them new things unless it's a pinafore or so at Christmas. Of course I make up everything I can get. I have a machine that I bought when I was single, and I've just made Tom a suit out of a pair of trousers his father couldn't wear a day longer. Look at him ! " We admired Tom in his comfortable outfit, and congratulated his mother.

" But the shoes—you can't get shoes given, and we're bound to have them," she lamented.

" How much will shoes cost you a year ? "

" Well, there's two pairs for my husband at 5s. each. These last him a bit over a year, with mending. The eldest boy buys his own shoes out of his pocket money. Herbert has to have two 4s. pairs. Then Violet has to have two pairs every year—that's 6s. And Bobbie has had three pairs, and the last is just worn out. They were 3s. 6½d., 2s. 11d., and 3s. 11d. Oh, and the mending won't come to less than 10s. a year. Then—I forgot myself—sometimes my sister sends me her old ones, but I got one pair this year at 4s. 6d. And the youngest "—she ran over various items rapidly in her mind— " he's cost 5s. for shoes."

" Are you very heavily in debt ? "

This was a poser. But Mrs. Abbott promised to look up all her old bills ; but she fancied that the sum of debt would not be less than £10. Yet the tradespeople had never worried her, knowing quite well that they would all be paid when two or three of the children began to earn.

She is a " contriving " woman. In the season

her boys go round gathering crabs and blackberries, and this year she bought a peck of plums
at 1s. and a peck of apples at 1s.

" I persevere, and go short of something when
fruit's round, for they're all fond of jam."

She has made 50 lbs. of jam this year, which
she uses at the rate of 2 lbs. weekly, or more
when she has a day's work, since then her husband and children, being deprived of potatoes,
eat all the more pastry.

Here, as in other cases, when vegetables are
got straight from the land, the amount con-
sumed varies. Here it is stated as $\frac{1}{4}$ peck potatoes per day. She uses six sacks a year. Less
greens are used, and it is not only a question of
the amount of them available—naturally if used
every day they would not last the year—but of
whether the housekeeper has time to prepare
them on a particular morning.

But nearly all families with large gardens or
allotments use greens or other vegetables twice
a week, and some three or four times. Potatoes
are generally used six days in the week ; but
often the Saturday's or the washing-day's dinner
is a " scratch meal."

There is a deficiency of 27 per cent. of protein in this family's dietary. One-twelfth of the food consumed is home produce.

EXPENDITURE DURING TYPICAL WEEK IN NOVEMBER 1912.

	s.	d.		s.	d.
52 lbs. bread . . .	5	11½	3 pints oil, and matches	0	4
2 lbs. dough, currants and lard (made into cake]	0	2¾	Soap, soda, starch . .	0	4
			Wood.	0	3
2 lbs. pastry lard . .	1	3	Blacking, laces . . .	0	1
1 lb. margarine . . .	0	8	Salt, mustard, pepper .	0	1
⅓ lb. currants . . .	0	2	Baking powder . . .	0	1½
2½ lbs. bacon . . .	2	0	Rent of allotment about	0	3½
2 lbs. shin beef . . .	1	0	Corn for fowls . . .	0	6
6 oz. tea	0	6	Man's insurance . .	0	3
¼ stone flour	0	11	Boy's pocket money, covering clothes and		
¼ lb. suet	0	1½	insurance	2	0
2¼ pints milk . . .	0	3½			
6 lbs. sugar	1	2		21	1¼
Tin gravy salt . . .	0	2	Balance towards rent,		
2 oz. pea flour . . .	0	1	clothing, and sun-		
¼ lb. cocoa	0	4½	dries	1	10¾
½ lb. cheese	0	4½			
1¼ cwt. coal	1	7	£1	3	0

HOME PRODUCE CONSUMED DURING THE WEEK.

21 lbs. potatoes.	3 lbs. carrots.
8¼ lbs. greens.	3 lbs. turnips.

	BREAKFAST.	DINNER.	TEA.	SUPPER.
SUN. .	Tea, bread and margarine.	Gravy pudding, potatoes, greens.	Tea, dough cake.	Meat, bread, cocoa.
MON. .	Tea, bread and margarine.	Suet pudding, potatoes, greens.	Tea, bread and margarine.	Bacon and bread, cocoa.
TUES. .	Tea, bread and margarine.	Bacon, potatoes.	Tea, bread and margarine.	Bacon and bread, cocoa.
WED. .	Tea, bread and jam.	Jam pudding, potatoes, greens.	Tea, bread and jam or lard.	Bacon and bread, cocoa.
THUR. .	Tea, bread and margarine or jam.	Soup, potatoes, greens.	Tea, bread and margarine or jam.	Bacon and bread, cocoa.
FRI. .	Tea, bread and jam or lard.	Suet pudding, carrots, turnips.	Tea, bread and margarine or jam.	Bread and margarine, cocoa.
SAT. .	Tea, bread and margarine or jam.	Potatoes, carrots, turnips.	Tea, bread and margarine or jam.	Bacon and bread, cocoa.

Man and son sometimes take a little bread and cheese with them to eat between breakfast and dinner.

Study No. XXXVIII.—West Riding
of Yorkshire.

Man, wife, two sons aged seven and three,
and two daughters aged ten and nine.

TOTAL WEEKLY EARNINGS OF FAMILY.

Wages—
Man	17	0
Wife	2	7½
	19	7½

Perquisites—
Cottage, garden, milk, and potatoes, say	3	7
	23	2½

Extra earnings in the course of the year, £1.

Mrs. Garrow is a busy, cheery housewife. She
is full of energy, and it gives her a real sense of
satisfaction to build up a healthy, happy home
life out of the materials to her hand.

They are well off for labouring people. Mr.
Garrow gets 17s. weekly, a free cottage and
garden, one quart of skimmed milk a day, and
sometimes potatoes. Last year, what with the
farmer's contributions and their own garden,
they bought no potatoes at all.

There is £1 extra at harvest, which is relied upon to furnish shoes and trousers for the husband. In spite of all these advantages, Mrs. Garrow tells us that she could not manage comfortably or adequately without her own earnings, which amount to rather over half-a-crown a week, taking one week with another.

Such a statement is significant, for her husband's earnings are high as agricultural earnings go. But it will be seen in the analysis of food consumed that this family is receiving an adequate amount of nourishment. Moreover, it is self-supporting. The united earnings of husband and wife provide not only food but clothing and all the necessaries of life. In short, they are above the level in which external help is necessary to maintain health and comfort.

Of course it must be remembered that Mr. Garrow is a thoroughly competent and reliable workman, and Mrs. Garrow somewhat more capable than the majority. She makes all the children's clothes herself, and she so calculates her expenditure as never to get into debt. Even the purchase of the minutest household sundries, such as black-lead and blacking, shoe laces, salt, matches, etc., is so adjusted as never to press too heavily upon the food bill. In fact, she is a born manager.

Wood is picked up by herself and the children. They are all on cordial terms with the farmer for whom Mr. Garrow works; and often when he is going on a quest for eggs, he takes little Bobby Garrow with him. This means an egg in the small boy's hand when he returns, and a Yorkshire pudding on Sunday. They never buy eggs.

When fruit is cheap Mrs. Garrow generally stews a good deal with a little sugar, to save buying jam; and this year there have been a few plums in the garden for pies. She calculates that she bakes about three-quarters of the stone of flour into pastry, as neither husband nor children would consider that they were equipped for work without it. Moreover, she herself goes out to work three times in the fortnight, and on these occasions solid chunks of pastry have to do duty for potatoes and pudding alike. She bakes twice a week, and is sufficiently progressive to use whole-meal as well as white flour.

This family's dietary shows almost exactly the amount of protein theoretically required to maintain physical efficiency, and an excess of 6 per cent. in the calories. Five per cent. of the food consumed is home produce, and about 9 per cent. is a perquisite.

EXPENDITURE DURING TYPICAL WEEK IN OCTOBER 1912.

	s.	d.		s.	d.
2 stones flour . . .	3	6	2 ducks (7 or 8 oz. each)	0	2
¼ stone whole-meal . .	0	5	1 lb. Quaker oats . .	0	3
2 lbs. lard	1	4	1½ cwt. coal	1	10½
1½ lbs. margarine . .	1	0	Insurance (State) . .	0	4
8 oz. tea	0	8	Insurance and clubs for		
2 lbs. jam	0	9	family	1	1
½ lb. currants . . .	0	2	To carrier	0	2½
1 lb. rice	0	2	Soap, soda, hearthstone	0	3
½ lb. sago	0	2	Oil, candles, matches,		
2 lbs. sugar	0	5	salt	0	4
6 lbs. beef, thick rib					
(frozen)	3	0		17	11½
2 lbs. cod	0	8	Balance for clothing and		
½ lb. suet	0	3	sundries	1	8
¼ lb. baking powder . .	0	2½			
4 oz. yeast	0	3		19	7½
1½ lbs. frozen sausages .	0	6			

HOME PRODUCE CONSUMED DURING THE WEEK.

13 lbs. potatoes.	⅓ lb. onions.
4 lbs. greens.	2 lbs. jam.

PERQUISITES CONSUMED DURING THE WEEK.
7 quarts skim milk.

	BREAKFAST.	DINNER.	TEA.	SUPPER.
SUN.	Tea, bread and margarine, sad cakes.	Beef, Yorkshire pudding, potatoes, greens.	Tea, bread and margarine, pastry.	Bread and margarine.
MON.	Tea, bread & margarine, meat (man), porridge (for children).	Beef, potatoes, boiled rice with currants.	Tea, bread and margarine, pastry.	Bread and margarine.
TUES.	Tea, bread & margarine, meat (man), porridge (for children).	Cold beef and bread, cold sago pudding.	Tea, bread and margarine, pastry.	Bread and margarine.
WED.	Tea, bread and margarine, pastry, "duck" (for man).	Hashed beef with onions, potatoes, greens, suet dumplings.	Tea, bread and margarine, pastry.	None.
THUR.	Tea, bread & margarine, "duck" (for man), porridge (for children).	Fish, potatoes, rice pudding.	Tea, bread and margarine, pastry.	None.
FRI.	Tea, bread & margarine, remainder of "ducks" (for man), porridge (children).	Beef pie, bread.	Tea, bread and margarine, currant tea-cakes.	Bread and margarine.
SAT.	Tea, bread and margarine, pastry.	Rice pudding, bread and margarine, tea.	Tea, bread, sausages and potatoes, pastry.	None.

The woman had dinner and tea on Tuesday and Friday at her employer's.

*Study No. XXXIX.—West Riding
of Yorkshire.*

Man, wife, two sons aged four and three, and
two daughters aged six and one.

TOTAL WEEKLY EARNINGS OF FAMILY.

	s.	d.
Man's wage	22	0
Perquisites—		
Cottage, garden, and 3 pints of milk		
a day, say	4	7½
	26	7½

At haytime and harvest the man gets his food given by
his employer.

The Barkers live in a cottage built into the
hillside, and heather and bracken grow nearly
down to its four walls. There is a good living-
room, a back-kitchen, a coal-house, and two
bedrooms.

The interior is more cheery than that of most
labourers' cottages. There is a pan of dough
on the fender before a bright fire, for it is baking
day. Mrs. Barker bakes twice a week. Two
little ones are playing round her, and a hen at the
open door is in search of possible bread-crumbs.

The village in which Mr. Barker works for a large dairy and cattle farmer is on the fringe of an active industrial region, and wages are high accordingly. He gets 22s. weekly, with the cottage free, and three pints of new milk daily. They keep poultry in the small garden and use their own eggs, and occasionally have a chicken for dinner on Sunday. There is no overtime money ; but during the haytime and the harvest all Mr. Barker's food is found, except on Sundays. But during this period the working days are very long — from 3 or 4 a.m. to 10 or 10.30 p.m.

On Sundays he is generally working about the farm most of the day, and when any of the cattle are ill he is often up all night. In the lambing season he is up regularly every alternate night. His employer is a man rapidly growing richer, who pays his men well but works them hard, and Barker's position is not altogether enviable, in spite of the 22s. weekly and perquisites. There are men in the same village earning only a pound a week who would not care to exchange with him.

" I'd rather have a pound and go a bit easier

than I'd have more and be driven to death," said one.

The heaviest item in the expenditure of the Barkers, which very materially reduces the money available for food, is insurance. At a certain age Mr. Barker will enter into the receipt of a regular benefit, while even now his wife would get £100 " if anything happened him "—the usual euphemism for death. But for these advantages they pay the premium, exceptionally high for a working man, of £7, 11s. 3d. yearly ; and Mrs. Barker always tries to put away the weekly fraction of this sum. This is why, with a menu more varied than that of most agricultural labourers, they only appear to " live like fighting cocks," but are really underfed.

There is a deficiency of 14 per cent. of protein in this family's dietary, and of 1 per cent. of energy value. The perquisites amount to nearly one-sixth of the food consumed, and an eleventh part is home produce.

EXPENDITURE DURING TYPICAL WEEK IN AUGUST 1912.

	s.	d.		s.	d.
1½ stones flour . . .	3	0	½ lb. hake for frying .	0	2½
4 oz. yeast	0	2	7 oz. pork chop . . .	0	3
18 oz. bread	0	2	3 lbs. stewing beef . .	1	10
2 sweet cakes . . .	0	2	½ lb. potted meat . .	0	3
1 lb. butter	1	0	½ stone potatoes . .	0	4½
1½ lbs. lard	0	11½	½ stone Indian corn . .	0	7½
1 lb. golden syrup . .	0	3	2 cwt. coal	2	0
4 lbs. sugar	0	10	Oil and firelighters . .	0	5
½ lb. tea	0	11	Soap	0	3
4 oz. baking powder .	0	2½	Stamps and picture		
¼ lb. ground rice . . .	0	1	post-cards	0	6
½ lb. rice	0	1½	Insurance (laid by		
½ lb. currants . . .	0	2	weekly)	3	0
2 oz. candied peel . .	0	1	State insurance . . .	0	4
1 lb. apples	0	2½			
½ lb. French beans . .	0	1½		20	8
2 small fruit jellies . .	0	2	Balance towards clothes,		
½ lb. blackberries. . .	0	1½	etc.	1	4
1 lb. cheese	0	8½			
1 lb. bacon	0	10		22	0
½ lb. corned beef . . .	0	4			

HOME PRODUCE CONSUMED DURING THE WEEK.

17 eggs. | 3 lbs. jam.

1 chicken.

PERQUISITES CONSUMED DURING THE WEEK.

21 pints new milk.

	BREAKFAST.	DINNER.	TEA.	SUPPER.
SUN. .	Tea, bread, bacon and eggs.	Chicken, potatoes, gravy, milk pudding.	Tea, bread, cheese, jam, tea-cakes.	Cold stewed beef and chicken, bread.
MON. .	Tea, bread, bacon and eggs.	Cold chicken and potatoes, tea, cakes.	Tea, bread and jam, cakes.	Tea - cakes, boiled eggs, tea.
TUES. .	Tea, bread, eggs, cheese.	Corned beef and potatoes, milk, cakes.	Tea, bread and butter or jam, tea-cakes.	Fish, bread and butter.
WED. .	Tea, bread, bacon (for man), eggs (for children).	Chop, beans, cakes, tea.	Tea, bread and butter, jam cakes.	Eggs, bread and jam.
THUR. .	Tea, bread, bacon (for man), eggs (for children).	Stewed beef, potatoes, rice pudding.	Tea, bread and jam, cakes.	Beef pie and tea (for man), jam and bread.
FRI. .	Tea, bread, eggs, potted meat.	Cold beef pie, potatoes, remainder of rice pudding.	Tea, bread and jam, cakes.	Tea, cakes.
SAT. .	Tea, bread, eggs and bacon.	Stewed meat, bread, tea, ground rice pudding.	Tea, jam and bread, pasties.	Bread and cheese, egg.

Only the man and wife have supper as shown; the children have bread and milk. The baby has bread and milk at each meal.

The children often have bread and milk or bread and jam between breakfast and dinner.

Study No. XL.—North Riding of
Yorkshire.

Man, wife, five sons aged fifteen, twelve, ten, seven, and five, and three daughters aged thirteen, three, and one month.

TOTAL WEEKLY EARNINGS OF FAMILY.

	s.	*d.*
Wages—		
Man	18	0
Son	2	6
	20	6

(The man pays 8s. per week for board and lodgings near to his work, coming home for week-ends. The eldest son sleeps at home, but gets all meals out, except Sunday night's supper.)

Rent of cottage and garden, £3, 10s. per year.

Extra earnings in the course of the year, £2, 10s.

Mr. and Mrs. Eyre live in a small, four-roomed cottage. They have nine children, ranging from seventeen years to four weeks. The eldest, William, is a farm hand twenty miles away, getting £16 a year and living in. The next boy, Horace, is fifteen, and is working with a farmer in the village. He gets all his food (except supper on Sunday night) and 11s. a month, but he sleeps at home, and his wage has to provide clothing, washing, mending, and all his personal expenses. None of the other children have yet left school.

Eyre is working nearly six miles from home, and only comes home for week-ends. In the summer his wage is £1 a week, but in the autumn it drops to 18s. Eight shillings of this goes regularly for his board and lodging when away, so that he is not much better off than if he were working in the village for his food and 9s. a week, as many men do in the neighbourhood.

The long tramp over the moors, too, is trying, especially in wet weather, when the ground is soaked, and " it's like walking through bags of wet soot."

But there is not a vacant cottage on the estate which employs him, and in his own village there is no regular work to be had.

The rooms are badly overcrowded, never less than nine at home, and ten at the week-ends. The boys all sleep together, and the girls, including the baby, with their parents.

They tell us in apology that next door it is more crowded still. Two families live there—

one upstairs, one down. They could afford separate cottages, but there are none to be had " for love or money." There are six in one family and seven in the other. One comprises man and wife, three young children, and a grandmother ; the other, a grandmother and her widowed daughter, with a girl and boys, some under, some over, fourteen.

But to return to Mrs. Eyre. She is a woman of forty-three, worn and harassed, but full of intelligence. Both she and her husband have thought and read a good deal, and when she understood that we were trying to find out how people really lived on the land, she was glad to help, and we filled up together a typical week's budget. Expenses lately had been some-what abnormal, owing to the arrival of the last baby. There had been 5s. for the nurse and 1s. 6d. for a woman who came and helped. On the other hand, various friends brought pud-dings, and the vicar brought 2s. 6d. But now things have resumed their normal course. In the winter they will be worse off, since additional coal will be needed, and probably there will be more off-time.

They have had some terribly rough times. Mrs. Eyre told us that once, when her husband was temporarily out of work, " the children used to crawl over me asking for cake (bread-cake), and I had none. Sometimes the older ones would go out after dusk and gather two or three turnips (steal them, if you call it so), and then we'd have some turnip mash."

They sold everything for which they could get a customer, including the good bedroom " suite " with which they had started married life, and her husband's volunteer trophies. But, even when things came to the worst, she would not write to her own people for help, though her father was an engine-driver, earning good money, and had often told her to appeal to him if in want. He is now dead.

At present, they are comparatively prosperous. Eyre, who is a thoroughly steady and competent fellow, has had regular employment for about a year, partly at making a fish-pond, partly at fencing and harvesting. The eldest lad pays part of the rent of £3, 10s. a year, but can do no more, as he himself has lately had to pay a doctor's bill. Recently, too, he

bought a bicycle, with which he cycles home once
a fortnight, getting dinner and tea with them on
the Sunday. His mother washes and mends for
him as well as for the lad working in the village.

The clothes of the family are a great problem.
If they did not sometimes get " cast-offs " they
could not manage. One friend, living at a distance, helps them regularly in this way. One
of the farm hands who works with Eyre gave
him a pair of old shoes, which have descended
to Mrs. Eyre. But lately she had to buy a pair
of shoes for her daughter from a traveller, and
these are not yet completely paid for. Again,
the second lad had recently to buy a pair of
clogs at the market town, and, as it was impossible for him to walk there in his old shoes,
he paid 6d. to the carrier, which raised the cost
of the clogs to 5s. 6d. And the whole 11s.
which he earns are really needed badly for
household expenses.

The next lad, aged twelve, is "such a ran-
sacking boy, tears his things all to bits." In
fact, he is a thorough boy who likes to go nut-
ting with other boys. But the effect on clothes
is disastrous.

At present, Mrs. Eyre wants to take the baby to be churched, but is prevented by the fact that she has nothing to wrap it in but an old cot blanket. She herself looks very ill, and is poorly clad. But everything and every one is profoundly respectable. These people may be blamed for having so many children, but one cannot help feeling that, if they could be properly fed, the more children brought up by such honest, hard-working, intelligent folk the better.

The garden is not large, and is chiefly laid out in potatoes, which this year have most of them been ruined. They have already—in October—eaten the last of them. A few poor cabbages are left. But Mrs. Eyre says that, since potatoes have become so dear, they will hardly be able to buy any this winter, even if Eyre keeps in work. Even now they are only having vegetables occasionally.

The house and garden are very exposed, and the house is extremely damp. Moreover, as Eyre is away all the week, there is really no one to make the best of the garden, such as it is.

" If Eyre *does* lose his work this winter," says his wife, " I shall make for the first seat on

Wharby Road." This is the popular idiom for going to the workhouse.

Early this year Mrs. Eyre's father died, and, as she and her husband had helped to pay his insurance, £4 or £5 came to them. This was nearly all spent in much-needed clothing.

In the winter they will be almost compelled to use two bags of coal, or, at the very least, a bag of coal and half a bag of cinders (at 7½d. a bag) each week. This will curtail the expenditure on food. And there are pretty sure to be some days when Eyre cannot get work. Mrs. Eyre counted six such days in November and December of last year, equivalent to a dead loss of 18s.

The cocoa mentioned in the budget will soon be given up. Mrs. Eyre only began to take it before her confinement.

Really none of them ever get enough of even the plainest food. Sometimes the " meat bill " has gone down to 6d. And to be reduced to dry bread is not at all infrequent.

In the summer, however, they often spend 1s. 6d. on meat, and get 3 lbs. of rice and oatmeal a week instead of 2 lbs. Summer is wel-

come in spite of the hard work which it involves
—but it is all too brief.

There is a deficiency of 26 per cent. of protein
in this family's dietary, and of 19 per cent. of
energy value. Only 1 per cent. of the food consumed is home produce.

EXPENDITURE DURING TYPICAL WEEK IN OCTOBER 1912.

	s.	d.		s.	d.
7 pints separated milk			¼ lb. tea	0	4½
and 7 gills new milk .	0	7	¼ lb. currants	0	1¼
¼ lb. suet	0	1	2 oz. cocoa	0	2¾
½ lb. liver	0	2	1 cwt. coal	1	3
2 lbs. shin beef . . .	1	0	1 quart paraffin . . .	0	2½
2½ stones flour . . .	3	11	Matches and candles . .	0	1½
3 oz. yeast	0	2	Soap and soda . . .	0	4
1 lb. butter	1	2	Man's board and lodg-		
2 lbs. oatmeal . . .	0	4	ing	8	0
2 lbs. rice	0	4			
2 lbs. sugar	0	5½		19	8½
¼ lb. lard	0	2	Insurance (man and		
¼ lb. baking powder . .	0	2½	woman)	1	1
2 lbs. treacle	0	5			
Salt	0	1		20	9½

HOME PRODUCE CONSUMED DURING THE WEEK.
3 lbs. potatoes.

MENU OF MEALS PROVIDED DURING THE WEEK.

	BREAKFAST.	DINNER.	TEA.	SUPPER.
SUN. .	Tea, bread and butter or treacle, porridge.	Stewed beef, potatoes, rice pudding.	Tea, bread and butter, currant pastry, shortcakes.	Tea, bread, butter, cake.
MON. .	Tea, bread and butter or treacle.	Baking powder cakes, tea, cocoa, bread and treacle.	Tea, powder cakes, bread and butter.	None.
TUES. .	Tea, bread and butter, porridge.	Boiled rice, tea, bread and butter or treacle.	Tea, powder cakes, with butter or treacle.	None.
WED. .	Tea, bread and butter or treacle.	Bread, butter or treacle, tea.	Tea, bread and butter or treacle.	None.
THUR. .	Tea, bread and butter or treacle, porridge.	Liver, suet pudding, bread and tea.	Tea, bread and butter or treacle.	None.
FRI. .	Tea, bread and butter or treacle.	Bread and treacle or butter, tea.	Tea, boiled rice, bread.	None.
SAT. .	Tea, bread.	Bread, tea.	Tea, bread and treacle or butter.	None.

The woman and two of her daughters sometimes have a cup of cocoa between breakfast and dinner.

Study No. XLI.—Oxfordshire.

Man, wife, three sons aged fifteen, thirteen, and four, and five daughters aged fourteen, twelve, ten, six, and six.

TOTAL WEEKLY EARNINGS OF FAMILY.

	s.	d.
Wages—		
Man	15	0
Wife	3	6
Son	4	0
Son	3	0
	25	6
Perquisites—		
Cottage and garden, say	2	0
	27	6

Extra earnings in the course of the year, 25s. (20s. earned by the man and 5s. by the son).

Rent of additional cottage, 1s. per week.

Rent of allotment, 14s. 4d. per year.

The Curwens occupy two adjoining cottages, for one of which they pay 1s. rent weekly; the other is free. By this arrangement they have four bedrooms, two living-rooms, and two attics, and, as there are ten of them at home, these are all pressed into service in one way or another.

They may be regarded as a typical example of how a thrifty, hard-working family can live when several members of the household are earning. The wages are low. Mr. Curwen only gets 15s. weekly, of which 1s. is deducted for the extra cottage. But the eldest son brings in 4s. and the second son 3s. weekly, while Mrs. Curwen earns 3s. 6d. regularly for looking after her husband's three brothers, none of whom have faced the responsibility of marriage on a weekly wage of about 14s.

Curwen works hard for his 15s.—from 5 a.m. to 7 p.m., with half an hour for breakfast and about three-quarters of an hour for dinner. He also goes twice on Sunday to look after the horses. Last year he only earned £1 by over-time, and the eldest son earned an extra 5s. There is no " Michaelmas money."

The eldest girl will soon go out into service ; but at present she is helping her mother with the care of the younger children. They are a bright, cheery family, full of pluck. Most of the vegetables they consume are home-grown, and they use a great many. Besides the garden, they rent an allotment at 14s. 4d. yearly. Some-

times manure is given by one of Curwen's bach-
elor brothers; sometimes they buy it. They
spend £1 a year on wood, which they get in
March in the " lot," and which they often burn
in the summer instead of coal.

There is no tobacco and no beer, unless Curwen should be treated. Shoes in this household
are a very heavy item—not less than £2 yearly
—even when Mrs. Curwen mends the children's
shoes with her husband's old " uppers." As
for clothing—in the past few months new suits
for the father and the second boy alone have
cost 32s. But Mrs. Curwen's own clothing consists of the cast-offs of some relative. If pence
are ever given to the children, they are not
spent on sweets but stored in the penny bank
towards new clothing in the summer. It is a
Spartan way of living, even now; but before
the boys began to earn, it must have been one
long and uncompromising Lent.

There is a deficiency of 16 per cent. of protein
in this family's dietary and of 3 per cent. of
energy value. One-tenth of the food consumed
is home produce.

EXPENDITURE DURING TYPICAL WEEK IN NOVEMBER 1912.

	s.	d.		s.	d.
68 lbs. bread	7	9½	2 cwt. coal and wood .	2	6
2 lbs. cheese	1	6	Soap, soda, starch, etc. .	0	6
½ lb. currants	0	2	Laces, blacklead, black-		
Salt	0	0½	ing	0	2
1½ lbs. beef steak and			Insurance	0	4
¼ lb. suet	1	1½	Rent of additional		
1 lb. bacon	0	9	cottage	1	0
4 bloaters	0	3	Newspapers	0	1
12 fresh herrings . . .	0	6			
1 lb. butter	1	3		23	9
1 lb. margarine . . .	0	8	Balance towards cloth-		
3 pints new milk . . .	0	4½	ing and rent of allot-		
10 oz. tea	0	10	ment	1	9
14 lbs. sugar	2	4			
8 lbs. flour	1	0		25	6
4 oz. pea flour . . .	0	2			
2 quarts oil	0	5			

HOME PRODUCE CONSUMED DURING THE WEEK.

40 lbs. potatoes. | 21 lbs. sprouts.

	BREAKFAST.	DINNER.	TEA.
SUN. . . .	Tea, bread and butter or margarine.	Gravy pudding (suet), potatoes, sprouts, suet pudding with currants.	Tea, bread and butter or margarine.
MON. . . .	Tea, bread and butter or margarine.	Meat out of Sunday's pudding, potatoes.	Tea, bread and butter or margarine, cheese for man and boy.
TUES. . . .	Tea, bread and butter or margarine.	Bacon, potatoes, sprouts.	Tea, bread and butter or margarine, cheese for man and boy.
WED. . . .	Tea, bread and butter or margarine.	Bloaters, potatoes.	Tea, bread and butter or margarine, bacon for man and boy.
THUR. . .	Tea, bread and butter or margarine.	Herrings, potatoes.	Tea, bread and butter or margarine, cheese for man and boy.
FRI. . . .	Tea, bread and butter or margarine.	Bacon for man and boys, bread and butter or margarine.	Tea, bread and butter or margarine.
SAT. . . .	Tea, bread and butter or margarine.	Tea, bread and cheese.	Tea, bread and scrape.

If any vegetables are left from Sunday's dinner they are eaten up at supper-time. The cheese is chiefly eaten by the man and boys. When their work does not allow them to come home at dinner-time they take bread and cheese with them, and have dinner at teatime.

Study No. XLII.—Essex.

Man, wife, five sons aged fifteen, fourteen, nine, six, and four, and two daughters aged eleven and two.

TOTAL WEEKLY EARNINGS OF FAMILY.

Wages—		s.	d.
Man		13	3
Son		9	0
Son		4	0
		26	3
Perquisites—			
Cottage and garden, say . . .		2	0
		28	3

Extra earnings in the course of the year, 30s.

Mrs. Birch is a tall, buxom, rosy-faced woman, active and capable in every fibre. Her husband is steady, hard-working, and reliable, and they have a large family of children, apparently as efficient as themselves.

" You have to think before you spend," says Mrs. Birch. " I consist my week's money before I touch a halfpenny." The word " consist " came out very emphatically, obviously being a shot at " consider."

During these winter months Mr. Birch's earnings only average about 13s. ; but there is a lad earning 9s., who gives his mother 7s. weekly, and another brings in 4s. They have the cottage free. This year there was 30s. extra money at harvest-time, but none at haytime.

There are nine of them to keep, except that the second boy gets breakfast and lunch out. The sons as yet earn nothing for overtime.

This family is not in debt to any extent, though the expenditure in the week given overbalanced the average income for last month by over 1s. Mr. Birch's pay for the last four weeks has been 11s., 12s., 15s., and 15s. respectively. Later on he will have 15s. pretty regularly, as he is a good, trustworthy fellow who gets the first chance with his employer of any work that is to be done.

The eldest son, who reserves 2s., will probably advance 1s. in any crisis. They all much prefer butter to margarine, but during the poorest months they generally use the latter, and may take to it any week for the sake of economy.

There is a deficiency of 2 per cent. of protein in this family's dietary.

One-thirteenth of the food consumed is home produce.

EXPENDITURE DURING TYPICAL WEEK IN DECEMBER 1912.

	s.	d.		s.	d.
58 lbs. bread	7	0	Oil, candles, matches .	0	6
1 stone flour	2	0	Man's insurance and		
10 lbs. sugar	1	8	clothing club . . .	0	8
⅓ lb. tea	0	9	2 oz. cocoa	0	2
1 lb. cheese	0	9	4½ lbs. flank beef and		
1 lb. bacon	0	9	½ lb. suet	2	6
½ lb. lard	0	4½	1½ lbs. pie pieces . . .	0	6
2 lbs. butter	2	6	2 oz. tobacco	0	7
4 pints new milk . . .	0	6			
2 lbs. beef sausages . .	1	0		25	0½
¼ lb. currants	0	1	Eldest boy's pocket-		
Baking powder and egg			money (including in-		
powder	0	3	surance and clothing).	2	0
1½ cwt. coal	2	0			
1 lb. Quaker oats . .	0	2		27	0½
Soap, washing powder .	0	4			

HOME PRODUCE CONSUMED DURING THE WEEK.

42 lbs. potatoes. | 24 lbs. greens.

2 lbs. onions.

MENU OF MEALS PROVIDED DURING THE WEEK.

	BREAKFAST.	DINNER.	TEA.	SUPPER.
SUN. .	Tea, porridge, bread and butter, bacon.	Suet pudding, greens, potatoes.	Tea, bread and butter, cake.	Bread, cheese, cocoa.
MON. .	Tea, bread and butter.	Tea, bread and butter.	Tea, cold meat, and potatoes.	None.
TUES. .	Tea, bread and butter.	Tea, bread and butter.	Tea, stew with onions, potatoes, and dumplings.	None.
WED. .	Tea, bread and butter.	Tea, bread and butter.	Tea, meat pieces, greens, and potatoes.	None.
THUR. .	Tea, bread and butter.	Tea, bread and butter.	Tea, stewed meat, potatoes and dumplings, onions.	None.
FRI. .	Tea, bread and butter.	Tea, bread and butter.	Tea, sausages, greens, potatoes.	None.
SAT. .	Tea, bread and butter.	Tea, bread and butter.	Tea, sausages, potatoes, and greens.	None.

The father and the eldest son take bread and cheese or bacon with them for dinner each day. The second son gets breakfast and dinner given by his employer.

Having now given detailed descriptions of the 42 families investigated, we may proceed to summarize some of the main conclusions to be drawn from an examination of their household budgets. The principal figures are presented in the following table :—

WAGES AND INCOMES.

From the preceding table it will be seen that the weekly money earnings of the families under review * vary from 10s. per week to 26s. 3d., and, with the addition of perquisites—assuming for cottage and garden a uniform rent of 2s.— from 10s. to 28s. 3d. In estimating these averages, no account has been taken of extra earnings from occasional overtime, harvest, and the like (which, however, are stated in Col. VIII.), since, as already mentioned, these are too often balanced by loss of wages through wet weather and other causes.

A glance at the map (facing title page) will show that the proportion of studies falling under the different wage groups, while not exactly coinciding with the general distribution of agricultural labourers' wages in 1907, may nevertheless be looked upon as fairly typical of the agricultural labouring population of England.

The exact family income is not always easy to estimate, since the woman's earnings—if any— and often the contributions of the children, are

* Not counting one married man who receives 9s. and his board.

10 a

irregular and difficult to check. In the table, however, the actual total earnings of the families during a typical week have been stated as nearly as they could be ascertained.

An analysis of the figures given in the table shows that—

8 families, with an average of 4·6 children, have incomes (including perquisites) of less than 15s., averaging 12s. 3d.

9 families, with an average of 4·3 children, have incomes of 15s. to less than 17s., averaging 15s. 8d.

12 families, with an average of 4·0 children, have incomes of 17s. to less than 20s., averaging 18s. 4½d. ; and

13 families, with an average of 5·3 children, have incomes of 20s. or over, averaging 22s. 9d.

The highest total income, including perquisites, is 28s. 3d. for a family with seven children. Here the man earns 15s. 3d., and two sons 9s. and 4s. respectively.

In nineteen of the forty-two cases the perquisites include a cottage, usually with a garden of fair size. Other perquisites, it will be seen, amount to very little, except in three cases where potatoes sufficient for the greater part of the year form part of the wage, and in four cases where a sufficient amount of milk for ordinary household purposes is given. In the case of one family where the man is boarded by the employer, we have assessed the value of his food at 8s. This method of payment, though it secures the health of the breadwinner, accentuates the poverty of his home.

ADEQUACY OF DIET.

In view of much recent discussion on the relative well-being of rural and urban workers receiving similar wages, it will be of interest to ascertain how far the remuneration of agricultural labourers, with such perquisites and gifts as they may receive during a typical week, and with the produce from their own gardens, suffices to maintain them and their families in a state of physical efficiency. For this purpose, the household budgets obtained have been carefully analyzed, and the nutritive value of the food consumed has been ascertained and compared with standard requirements.

The amount of food necessary to maintain people in a state of physical efficiency varies with their age, sex, and the muscular severity of their work. In estimating the sufficiency of the diets, we have adopted Professor Atwater's standard of the food requirements of men engaged in " moderate " work — namely, 125 grammes of protein and 3,500 calories of energy value per man per day, with the proportionate amounts for women, and for children according to age.* We are, of course, aware that the science

* Until recently, the quantity of food required for the maintenance of physical efficiency was stated in terms of protein, fats, and carbohydrates ; but latterly, science has shown that all three are more or less interchangeable in the economy of the human body. It is simpler, therefore, to state the quantity of food required in terms of protein and potential energy or energy value. We have to state the protein separately, as a certain amount is requisite in every diet for building up muscle and tissue. But given this quota of protein for building purposes, it then becomes a matter of indifference, within reasonable limits, whether the potential energy required by the body is obtained from further protein, from fats, or from carbohydrates. The potential energy of food is usually stated in heat units or calories, the " larger calorie," which is the amount of heat required to raise 1 kilogramme of water 1° C. (or 1 pound of water 4° F.), being the one generally adopted. In thus expressing the potential energy of food it is not, of course, implied that all its potential energy takes the form of heat, but only that if it were converted into heat a certain number of calories or heat units would be produced.

1 gramme of protein yields 4·0 calories.
1 gramme of fats yields 8·9 calories.
1 gramme of carbohydrates yields 4·0 calories.

of dietetics is still in its infancy, and that authorities disagree as to the amount of nutriment
necessary to maintain physical efficiency. Careful
inquiry has, however, satisfied us that Professor
Atwater's standards are still the most reliable.
If it be urged that they are too high, we would
point out that we have not adopted his standard
for men engaged on "hard work," but only
that for men engaged on "moderate work;"
for work equivalent to that, say, of a house
painter. In doing so, we have probably under-
estimated the severity of the work undertaken
by agricultural labourers, especially when the
length of their working days is borne in
mind.*

Columns XI. and XII. of the table show the
relation of the food actually consumed by the
forty-two families to Professor Atwater's stand-

* According to Professor Atwater, the daily food requirements of
men are as follows :—

	PROTEIN (grammes).	ENERGY VALUE (calories).
For those engaged on—		
Light work	112	3,000
Moderate work . . .	125	3,500
Hard work	150	4,500

For further particulars as to the exact methods by which the
sufficiency or otherwise of a dietary may be ascertained, see B. Seebohm Rowntree's "Poverty," p. 223 et seq.

ard of requirements. It will be seen that the amount of protein obtained does not in a single case exceed that standard ; it just attains to it in one case—that of a Yorkshire family with four children, having a united income, including perquisites, of 23s. 2½d., and nearly approaches it in one other where the income and perquisites of an Essex labourer's family with seven children come to 28s. 3d. Unfortunately, the total number of family budgets investigated is not large enough to allow of their being graded closely according to income, so as to show with accuracy just how the degree of underfeeding decreases as the wages rise. The result of such a classification would only be trustworthy if the number of families investigated were very great, as otherwise exceptional circumstances affecting two or three families in each group are liable to render average figures unreliable. For instance, in three cases of very poor families we investigated, the gift of a pint of new milk a day materially raised the nutritive value of the dietary. In the case of the family with the highest wage of which we have a record, the quite exceptional sum of 3s. a week was spent on insurance. The keeping of pigs and poultry in some cases obscured the wage issue. Again, some budgets were taken in the winter, when coal was a heavy item, some in the early autumn. In some, the family is living largely on produce from their garden. In others, there is no garden, or its produce is exhausted. In one case a comparatively adequate wage is heavily mortgaged by weekly payments for debt. In other cases, children who have left home pay the rent for their parents. Thus an accurate picture of the actual facts can only be obtained if each case is considered separately.

But although no detailed classification is possible, the table shows that *the average shortage of protein of the forty-eight families is 24 per cent.;* and on the whole the underfeeding, as might be expected, is most serious in the case of the lowest wages. For those earning less than 15s., including perquisites, the average deficit of protein is 35 per cent., while for those earning 20s. and over it is 19 per cent.

If energy value be taken as the standard, we find that the average deficiency is 10 per cent. A sufficiency of it is obtained in ten cases, and the greatest deficiency occurring is one of 42 per cent. The average deficiency of the families with a wage of less than 15s., including perquisites, is 20 per cent., while for those with 20s. and over it is only 5 per cent.

It was, of course, to be expected that the deficiency of energy value would be less than that of protein, since the foods providing the former are cheaper than those providing the latter. But as an adequate supply of protein is an essential of physical efficiency, it is not incorrect to say that *on the average the forty-two families investigated are receiving not much more than three-fourths of the nourishment necessary for the maintenance of physical health.* And this is in spite of the fact that some of them are in receipt of substantial charity, while a great part of the incomes of others consists of supplementary earnings by wife or children.

The fact that so many of the families are underfed must not be taken as indicating that we have selected an undue proportion of those in receipt of low wages. It is unfortunately true that even in the districts where the highest wages are paid, such wages are still insufficient to provide a family of six or seven persons with the food necessary for full physical efficiency.

The physiological results of a scanty supply of protein are described by Dr. Robert Hutchison ("Food and the Principles of Dietetics," pp. 23–169), who says that—

> "the daily consumption (of protein) should never be allowed to sink below 100 grammes, but should preferably be 125. . . . It is well to have an excess of proteid above that barely required for tissue repair. To live on a minimum of proteid is to run the risk of having what one may call 'threadbare tissues,' and of having no reserve for use in emergencies. And such a condition of things makes for low resistance and for disease. There is also reason to believe that proteid, besides acting as a repairer of tissues and a source of energy, exerts upon the cells a stimulating influence which increases vitality and energy. A deficiency of it, too, seems to impair the condition of the blood, and lower the tone of the muscles and of the heart, besides enfeebling the digestive powers by restricting the supply of

the material from which the digestive ferments are elaborated. . . . The difference, in fact, between an animal fed on highly-nitrogenous diet and one supplied with little nitrogen is the difference between a steam-engine at half-pressure and one which is producing its full horse-power. . . . To growing children a deficiency of proteid in the diet is specially disastrous, for the lack of building material which it entails may result in impaired growth and development, the consequence of which may last throughout life. For the same reason, persons who habitually live on a minimum of proteid are apt to convalesce but slowly after an acute illness ; for, once their tissues are broken down, they have no ready surplus of building material out of which to repair them."

The foregoing extract shows how serious are the consequences of underfeeding such as we have noted in the case of the families investigated. They would have been still worse off but for the fact that the majority of the households were in a position to supplement the food purchased with product from their own gardens.

But the value of the garden to the labourer, important though it is with present money wages, must not be overrated. Less than a twelfth of the food consumed by these families was derived from their gardens. And it must be remembered that from a garden of the usual size produce cannot be obtained the whole year round.

There are many complaints that the labourer's wife is un-economical, but a study of the dietaries recorded does not support such a view. The fact that in many budgets part of the food consumed was home-grown and part received as a perquisite or a gift makes it impossible to estimate the economy or otherwise of the dietaries by ascertaining the amount of nutriment purchased with each shilling ; but it is interesting to note that only one-fifth of the nutriment is obtained from animal sources. This proportion is a trifle lower than in the case of a number of unemployed urban workers, who, on account of lack of resources, were for the time forced to live as economically as they possibly could,*

* "Unemployment," by B. S. Rowntree and B. Lasker (Macmillan, 1911), p. 225.

and much lower than in the case of a number
of urban workers with wages under 26s., where
it averaged about one-third.*

Meat of some description figures in all but
one of the dietaries; but, as already explained,
it often represents a flavouring rather than a
substantial course. " For the man only " is a
remark found in many of the menus.

Of milk, again, the under-consumption, especially in the households with many small children, is very serious, though sometimes the lack
of fresh milk is partly made up for by the purchase of condensed milk. In one of the forty-
two households no milk at all is consumed; in
fifteen only condensed, skimmed, or separated;
and in the twenty-six households where fresh
milk is part of the dietary, it only amounts to
an average of 5½ pints per family of two adults
and five children per week, or less than a pint
a day for each family.

The idea that country dwellers have facilities
for obtaining country produce not possessed by
those who live in towns is further contradicted
by the fact that butter does not figure at all in

* " Poverty," p. 240.

twenty of the forty-two budgets; dripping or margarine being used instead (the latter probably made in a Dutch factory). In only two cases is butter bought at a cheap rate from the employer.

One other point remains to be mentioned—namely, that the women and children suffer from underfeeding to a much greater extent than the men. It is tacitly agreed that the man must have a certain minimum of food in order that he may be able to perform the muscular work demanded of him; and the provision of this minimum, in the case of families with small incomes, involves a degree of underfeeding for the women and children greater than is shown by the average figures we present. It is not necessary to dwell on the short-sightedness of a policy which provides energy for the workers of to-day at the heavy cost of the growing children and of the women during their child-bearing period, the time of greatest financial stress in the life of the workers.

OTHER EXPENSES.

Very little need be said about the other items
of household expenditure, because they are almost insignificant compared with that on the
" daily bread." Twenty-four of the families
pay rent which, on the average, amounts to
1s. 10d. a week. Thirteen families, besides, pay
rent for an allotment, averaging 9s. 8d. per annum, equal to about 2d. per week. We have
no reason, as regards either, to complain that
they do not get their " money's worth." The
deplorable fact is that the payment of even
such low rents as most of those recorded often
involves encroachments upon the daily necessaries of life.

The amount actually spent on clothing in the
course of the year cannot be stated with any
accuracy. The descriptions show the many
makeshifts adopted to lay up a sufficient sum, now
and then to provide the breadwinner with a
new pair of working boots or to find shoes for
the children. But without the kindliness of
richer neighbours, grown-up children in service,
or relations who send occasional parcels, many

of the families under review, in the words of the Yorkshire woman (Study **XVIII.**), would " hae ter black theirsels ower an' go naykt."

Next in importance comes expenditure on sickness. The appalling burden of debt incurred by so many of these families at times of sickness suggests that, whatever the merits or demerits of the measure recently passed into law, some provision for insurance against this contingency cannot but be of immense benefit to the agricultural labouring class.

On going through the whole of the weekly balance sheets and extracting every item of expenditure upon luxuries, the exceeding slenderness of these outgoings is revealed. The term " luxury " is, of course, an elastic one, since such items as marmalade or condiments may by some be considered as such, and a weekly newspaper a necessary of modern life, whereas others might take the opposite view. But here we have defined it as including everything apart from food, household sundries, rent, clothing, medicine, and insurance ; and we find that the amount spent in this way per week only averages about 6d. per family, or $\frac{3}{4}$d. per person.

If out of this we allow the labourer 3½d. for a weekly ounce of tobacco (and few of us would grudge him what he often seems to look upon as his one solace), there is 2½d. left to supply the household with newspapers, stamps, books, railway fares—indeed, with any kind of luxury or recreation which costs money. But it must be borne in mind that, in nearly all cases, even our sixpenny average has been obtained by docking a food supply which is already inadequate.

Let the reader try for a moment to realize what this means. It means that from the point of view of judicious expenditure, the be all and the end all of life should be physical efficiency. It means that people have no right to keep in touch with the great world outside the village by so much as taking in a weekly newspaper. It means that a wise mother, when she is tempted to buy her children a pennyworth of cheap oranges, will devote the penny to flour instead. It means that the temptation to take the shortest railway journey should be strongly resisted. It means that toys and dolls and picture books, even of the cheapest quality, should never be purchased ; that birthdays should be practically indistinguishable from other days. It means that every natural longing for pleasure or variety should be ignored or set aside. It means, in short, a life without colour, space, or atmosphere, that stifles and hems in the labourer's soul as in too many cases his cottage does his body.

CHAPTER IV.

THE LABOURER'S OUTLOOK.

This short study cannot be fitly concluded without some attempt to analyze the general outlook of the agricultural labourer. Is his attitude one of content or discontent, of pure lethargy, of patient endurance, or of hope ? A great many people outside his own sphere are thinking a great deal about him, but what is *he* thinking, and what is he feeling ?

There is no escape from the answer. Not only in those districts where wages are at their lowest, but in the better paid districts, and among the labourers whose work is most regular, there is a profound dissatisfaction with things as they are, and a deepening conviction that, unless some vital change takes place, they will go from bad to worse. And in many cases this conviction is not merely personal or local, but is accompanied by the sense of a dangerous malady eating into the national life.

In the following pages we have tried to set down the main causes for this despondency and unrest, which seem to indicate that agriculture has either arrived at a hopeless *impasse* or the parting of the ways.

Relation between Farmers and Men.—To judge from local impressions, the farmers and their men in many English villages seem to be drifting further apart. Sometimes one finds the former days looked back upon half regretfully on either side ; though money wages were lower, there was more payment in kind, and on the whole a greater sense of comradeship. To quote one old farmer of a fine type, a humane, open-handed man :—

" I used to take an interest in my men ; but now I don't seem to care a snap about them, and I don't think they care a snap about me."

" We were taught in school to fear God and to help one another," said a north-country farmer. " Now it isn't ' how can you help a man ? ' but ' what can you mak' out on 'im ? ' And if your aim isn't to do men good, but to mak' money out on 'em, you've to put your conscience in your pocket and keep it close."

Of course many farmers blame the men for any decrease of cordiality, and complain, not without bitterness, that the latter are spoiled as workmen by a discontent, not inherent in their circumstances, but engrafted and fostered from without.

" If Wat Tyler came to-day, he could get no one to follow him," said one farmer, himself a kindly, well-educated, and sincerely religious man. " The men have no real grievances."

He declared that he himself was in pretty close touch with his men's actual requirements, and made every effort to meet them ; but that now artificial grievances were being manufactured and scattered broadcast, with the result that men were daily becoming less efficient and more grasping. And no cordial relationship could be established with people only eager to " get as much as they could for doing as little as they could." His opinion was sincere, and doubtless he could have supported it by many illustrations. But we could hardly help thinking that he would have been rather sorry to measure his own needs by the needs of his men. He took it for granted that he and they represented two different types of being, and thus he failed to grasp their point of view.

One of his own cattlemen, for instance, complained that he had been working for a couple of years without a single Sunday off. Not that he objected to Sunday work—it was part of the bargain—but he objected to it without a break, year after year. He could not get away for a week-end or even take his children for an outing. And this, to him, was a real grievance, especially as the working day began at 4 a.m.

The complaint of the men generally is similar to that of the farmers; but it is voiced with rather more bitterness. According to them, it is the masters who demand too much and give too little, who are indifferent to the welfare of the other party in the contract. Perhaps all the charges are best summed up in the one charge of indifference. It is alleged that the farmer's men are becoming mere machines to him, to be scrapped without reluctance when they cease to be profitable. He cares little how they live, or into what state their cottages fall; he makes no effort to keep them off the " Board," and so forth.

When it is suggested that perhaps farmers cannot afford to pay more wages or to look after their men more adequately, the answer in many districts takes the form of some such question as :—

" Why do they go on buying more land if farming don't pay ? "

" Why do they live as they do ? "

" Why do they buy motors and hunters ? "

They are often charged with forsaking a simple and hardworking life for one of greater ease and ostentation, the increased cost of which must be borne by the labourer.

There is no need in these pages to try to reconcile the divergent points of view represented by the master and the man, or to hold a brief for either. Nor do we ignore for a moment the many instances in which the relation between the two is absolutely cordial. We only wish to chronicle an impression that, speaking generally, the conflict of interests between the two classes is becoming more acute, and this is one of the causes underlying the labourer's discontent.

Under-Farming.—Another source of discontent lies in the inadequate cultivation of the soil in many districts. There is no doubt that " under-farming " is often looked upon by the workers in the light of a personal injury. Again and again one is struck by the intimate feeling of the labourer towards the soil.

" They ought to look after the land. Ain't she the mother of us all ? " said one man. An old woman who had never left her native village echoed it with,—

" What was the land sent for, if it wasn't for the poor to live off of ? "

Another, speaking of the property of a neighbouring farmer, said,—

" It's God's land, ain't it, not his'n."

The extent to which machinery has superseded labour is regarded by the worker as a calamity, but not as a wrong. Like the decline of small rural industries, it is accepted as the inevitable result of progress. But inadequate draining, fencing, walling, weeding, stoning, etc., land lying waste that might employ labour, " starved land," land suffered to " go all to pieces," or turned into " mere rabbit warrens "—these are crimes against the community, and against the land itself—crimes which rob labour of its legitimate sphere and frustrate the bounty of nature.

Of course the farmer is not necessarily the culprit. He is often severely handicapped. Apart from questions of security of tenure, it is well known that competition for farms sometimes raises their rent beyond the figure which a farmer can really afford; and it may sometimes, from the purely selfish point of view, and balancing one risk against another, be his actual interest to " farm to leave." But wherever the blame lies, this under-cultivation of the soil is partly responsible for the gloomy outlook of the agricultural labourer.

The Feudal Danger.—No doubt in many parts of the country this under-cultivation does not exist. There are still " estates like gardens," and landowners who are in no sense of the word absentees. The old feudal relationship has not completely disappeared, and we feel strongly disposed to think that from a material point of view the labourer directly or indirectly under the sway of some paternal if autocratic landed proprietor is better off than the labourer in

some " independent " village, where the land is
split up into small struggling freeholds. He
often has a higher standard of comfort, and feels
vaguely conscious of what in the towns we call
" a grip on society," through some influential
person. But it would be idle to ignore that
these things represent another kind of danger—
the danger that the individual may himself
become part of the estate. And this danger is
often realized keenly. We repeatedly found villages in which the farms were poor, the work
was precarious, and everything had a forlorn
and " out-at-elbows " aspect, glorying in their
superiority over some adjacent village whose
inhabitants were better housed and better fed
but " couldn't call their souls their own."

The Rising Generation.—But whatever may be
the point of view of the labourer living more or
less under the feudal system, there is no doubt
that in an appalling number of cases the worker
in the country feels that he and his are steadily
losing ground. It is not only a question of employment here and now; it is a question of the
future of the family. Ask any village mother
who is ambitious for her boys where she wants

them to spend their lives. The answer is generally,—

   " Not on the land—there's nothing for them."

Doubtless many boys begin to work on farms even before they leave school, and pass from school to " living in." But this is looked upon rather as a prelude to adventure in the towns or in the colonies than as a final choice. Not that the lot of the farm-hand living in is without advantages. He is often better housed and fed than his own father and mother. But it must be remembered that his comparative comfort only lasts while he is single. Marriage is a desperate risk. It is risky even when he has saved something towards the furnishing of a cottage or the purchase of a pig—and is allowed to keep a pig and fortunate enough to find a cottage. But, as one north-country labourer put it, " the farm man who marries without having saved anything is done." And in many cases the claims upon him of father and mother and younger brothers and sisters make it impossible for him to save. Meanwhile, beyond the narrow limits of the village there are not only adventures, but the hope and possibility of a successful life. And so it comes to pass that all over the country there are vicars interested in their flocks, schoolmasters eager for their pupils, who make it one of their main objects to secure situations on the railway or in some urban area for all their smart, promising lads.

The girls, too, leave home. The complaint is made occasionally that the few residential people of the village have a growing distaste for employing girls whose homes are close by, and who on any and every occasion may want to run home, presumably to gossip. However much or however little truth there may be in that statement, there is no doubt that innumerable girls go into service in towns when they are too young and inexperienced to look after themselves, and most need home care. But not all parents, much as they would prefer to keep their girls within reach, can afford to " hold on " till a suitable situation is forthcoming in some adjacent village. They must at all risks dispense with the burden upon their resources of an inmate who is old enough to earn and yet is earning nothing. Only if there should be work in the village for the mother, for which she is set free by her daughter's care of the children, is the evil day deferred.

" There isn't a girl in the village besides me," said one bright young woman of eighteen, who was keeping house for her brother and grandfather, her mother being dead. " They've all gone away somewhere—into service mostly." And naturally the most intelligent lads and girls, the most energetic young men and women, are the first to leave. It is the dull boy or anæmic girl, the mature worker without talent or without initiative, who remains in the village, " existing, not living."

It may naturally be asked, " But what about field work ? " The answer is that, partly owing to the introduction of machinery in many parts of England, field work is no longer an industry that can support a girl at home. And in those regions where it amounts to an occupation for half the year, the effect on the *morale* and character of those engaged in it is far from beneficial. Especially, of course, is this the case when the denizens of the slums of the nearest large town and the women and girls of the village are brought into daily contact, or there is too much rough familiarity between the boys and girls. We do not wish to imply that there is no scope for women's labour in the lighter kinds of field work ; but as carried on at present in any large market-gardening region—and nowhere else is it a substantial source of income —it is often more of a curse than a blessing.

Monotony.—The real reason of the drift of the young people from the villages is not, as is often contended, the superior attractions of the towns. " They go because there's nothing here," is the constant explanation. But doubtless the fascination of the town, when once experienced, disqualifies them for the old life.

It must be remembered that poverty and monotony go hand in hand. To take a trivial instance, one labourer's wife who was comparatively well off, as she had a husband and sons working, and worked herself, said that for three or four of them to go to a " public concert," which had been got up by some local magnate and was to be held in the schoolroom, was quite impossible, as the tickets were 6d. each. Two other cases of village concerts at this pro-

hibitive price came under our notice. They
seem to point to a lack of realization, even on
the part of those who are sincerely anxious to
provide some recreation for the people, of the
extreme slenderness of their resources. Again,
over and over, even when there was a comfortable reading-room in the village, we found that
the minute subscription needed to keep a man
within its benefits had lapsed in favour, not of
drink, but the necessaries of life. The same thing
often happens with regard to cricket or football
clubs in districts in which wages are admittedly
inadequate. Even the collecting box at church
or chapel may be an unwelcome tax. " You
can't go without giving a halfpenny," said one
poor soul ruefully. To be sure, there is always
a chance of gossip with a neighbour or a friend,
or sometimes even a game of cards in the winter
evenings. And those evenings are brief. Work
in the open air, especially when the hours are
those of horsemen or cowmen, and combined, as
it often is, with necessary economy in the matter
of oil and fuel, frequently means " bed at eight
o'clock, and glad to get there." The worker has
little time in which to complain of monotony,

but this does not make life less monotonous. He is starved mentally and emotionally; his perfectly healthy craving for simple pleasure is starved.

It may be contended, of course, that he derives much comfort from his daily contact with Nature and the contemplation of the clouds and the stars. He may—no doubt he does ; but it is a subject upon which we have no definite statistics. Our own impression is that when the utmost allowance has been made for the value of his communion with Nature, his life will still be gray. As for the pipe and the alehouse, rate them at their utmost worth, and they are only narcotics, not giving positive value to life, but deadening its vague discomfort.

Religious Outlook.—It may reasonably be asked what the churches have done or are doing to make the labourer's life worth while. It is difficult to answer this question. In some of the villages we visited the feeling of the poorer people towards the churches seemed to be one of indifference, if not of half-resentful scorn. Organized religion was outside their daily life. On the other hand, we know that many clergymen are doing their very utmost to help and inspire the people among whom they live and work, not only on Sundays, but throughout the week. We know, too, that the little chapel is often a real escape from the monotonous struggle. Yet it would be idle to deny that the full enjoyment of the social aspects of Christian fellowship, whether in church or chapel, the tea meeting, the harvest thanksgiving, the missionary meeting, is not for the very poor, but for those who can co-operate actively by gifts of money or of kind. A great spiritual awakening is needed before, even in the church, the poor can entirely lose the feeling that " they are beaten every way."

The Cottage.—But after all, it may be said that the home is the first consideration. And surely here the agricultural labourer has many advantages. We think of the Christmas almanac cottage, with its old-fashioned borders and ivy-clad walls, its roses climbing round the porch. There are such cottages ; but we remember vividly an interview with an old age pensioner who lived alone in such an one. The interior was as picturesque as the exterior, with a quantity of old china displayed on the dresser. But it was extremely dark and extremely damp, and a rat was part tenant.   One turns from such cottages with actual relief to hideous brick erections, whose windows are a trifle larger, and whose walls are a trifle less mouldy.

As for the cottages which furnished our budgets, they might very often have been transplanted, singly or in rows, from some cheerless little street in a sordid city area.   And the old-fashioned flowers which we associated with village life had apparently, to a very great extent, yielded precedence to potatoes.   As for the roses climbing round the porch—in the first place there were no porches, and in the second no one would ever have time or patience to make roses climb about them.   These decorative features are less characteristic of the poorly-paid labourer's cottage than of the house and garden of the successful farmer or the well-paid artisan residing in the country.   But after all that is a minor detail.   The real trouble is the lack of adequate cottages.   Many young people for whom work could be found in the village leave because it is impossible to find a roof to shelter

11 *a*

them.   On the one hand, there is overcrowding;
on the other, numberless cottages are falling
into ruin because no landlord finds it worth
his while to repair them at the rent.   And summer visitors flocking in from the towns, though
they quicken the rural life and give a little employment, still more complicate the housing
problem.   What cottages there are, as a rule,
do not suffice for the needs of a growing family—
and it seldom occurs to the agricultural labourer
and his wife to limit the number of their household.   Sometimes, indeed, they seem to regard
their children as an asset, a kind of insurance of
which they will get the benefit when once they
are old enough to earn.   However this may be,
the ordinary four-roomed cottage is insufficient.
The second room downstairs is often a mere
scullery, and as for the second bedroom, in the
words of one villager, " You fit into it as you
will one day into your coffin."

And very often an inadequate water supply
is added to inadequate housing.   Sometimes the
well is a quarter of a mile distant; sometimes in
dry weather it is impossible to get enough water
for washing purposes.   Over one well, supplying

a cluster of cottages, we came across the legend,
" This water should be boiled before drinking."
The local explanation was that the drainage from
some large residential houses standing at a
higher level filtered into the spring.

The Garden.—The industrial worker, earning
perhaps 20s. a week, in a crowded urban area
sometimes longs wistfully for the life-giving
breezes of the country and the unlimited supplies of garden produce. He dreams of hens
and pigs, possibly even cows; and he does not
realize the real limitations of the agricultural
worker's lot. Gardens are certainly a tremen-
dous asset, without which a great many people
simply could not live. But as a rule they must
be supplemented by allotments; and even when
the produce of the allotment is added to that of
the garden, families are seldom supplied with
potatoes the whole year round. As for the more
nutritious garden stuff, such as peas or beans,
it is regarded as more or less of a luxury. Potatoes are the staple food which is relied on to
eke out bread.

Doubtless if more work were put into the
gardens or allotments, and more money ex-

pended on seeds or manure, they would yield more. But those who most need garden produce are often most heavily handicapped as regards both capital and time. Take, for example, a labourer with wife and five children, earning 14s. a week and a free cottage. In view of the necessities of his growing family he has taken a place as cowman or horseman to earn that "free" cottage. He has to begin work at 4 or 5 a.m. all the year round, works perhaps till between 5 and 6 p.m., and often has to go back last thing to "fodder up." He also works on Sundays. Such a man has not a great deal of spare time for gardening; nor has he much capital to invest in seeds, manure, and tools. And in many parts of England his condition is perfectly typical. One such man, a sturdy, indefatigable person, said that he had often "gardened by moonshine." He had four children, and worked long hours as a horseman. But he also did cobbling, sometimes working till eleven at night; and the cobbling paid, among other things, for seeds and for tobacco. But one can hardly expect every labourer to be so strenuous, or to have an additional trade in his hand; and in the majority of cases, though the men do work at their own gardens after hard days, when they are "fit to drop," they are hardly likely to extract the utmost value from them.

But the pig—and the hens? With respect to these, we must not forget that labourers whose work is among horses or cattle are seldom allowed to keep pigs. But we came across several cases in which, owing largely to the increased price of meal, labourers who had formerly kept pigs had given up doing so. As a matter of fact, however, it is generally the women who look after pigs and hens. And their energy, if they have any left after making and mending for their families, very often flows in the direction of some occupation whereby a weekly shilling or two can be earned in cash. "It's no use hungering yourself to keep a pig," said one; while for the very poorest, the purchase of the pig is an insuperable obstacle. Even the enterprise of keeping poultry is beyond them. Apart from the initial cost of the hens, they cannot turn the garden into a hen-run; and even 6d. a week for their food is a heavy item.

Other Supplementary Resources.—But what about other supplementary resources ? No doubt additional earnings by various members of the family often mitigate the severity of the struggle to live on an inadequate wage. We found on one occasion that in three small villages only one man and woman with a small family were actually living on the wage of a day-labourer. In another case the woman took in washing ; in another the husband was sexton as well as labourer ; while one family had " got through the worst." They were left heavily in debt, but the children had begun to earn. But it must be remembered that supplementary earnings are least available when they are most needed—in the child-bearing period.

Again, there are villages in which the bolder and more wayward create purple patches in their lives, and augment inadequate wages by stealing—a turnip, a little corn, some hay, a rabbit, or a chicken. Physically, their families are healthier than those of people who do not steal. But they suffer in more subtle ways, and the very atmosphere of the village seems to alter for the worse.

The inadequacy of the wage is obscured, further, by charitable gifts or the help of relatives. These most frequently take the form of cast-off clothing. It is difficult to realize the extent to which even families in which the bread-winner is earning a comparatively high wage are only enabled to keep up a respectable appearance by the gifts of richer people, or relatives in a slightly better position. Their incomes, especially in a village with rare jumble sales and no opportunities of picking up cheap bargains, simply do not run to clothes. The self-supporting family in this connection is painfully rare. And yet, in countless instances, even when the labourer with wife and children has earned a free cottage or an additional shilling, at the cost of overwork, and when all the sources from which the meagre wage can be augmented have been rated at their full worth, the fact remains that he and his are still underfed. And, as has elsewhere been suggested, the wife and the children are the first to suffer.

Consanguinity.—Before concluding, we may touch briefly on one more danger which the drift away from the country is rendering more grave. It is the danger of constant intermarriage, and the consequent weakening of originally healthy families. A well-known medical officer of health told us that one village problem which he was continually facing was the prevalence of consanguinity with its attendant evils. He had analyzed with great care the population of two adjacent villages, and found that consanguinity brought in its train many other evils. Out of 140 school children in the two villages, 102 were related more or less closely. Of these, 14 were mentally deficient, 12 extremely dull, 2 very defective in speech, 2 deaf and dumb, 20 illegitimate. In recent years there had been two suicides and three cases of insanity among the older relatives of these children. Such facts are very far from being isolated.

Taking together all these aspects of the life of the agricultural labourer, can we be surprised at his despondent outlook? It may be asked if he has no faith in political or trade-union machinery. As regards the first, he seems to be as destitute of faith in politics as of faith in theology; but as regards the second, he honours, even if he cannot see his way to following, the policy of combination. Here and there we meet a man who has tried to keep a union alive and has been baffled. And of course it is impossible for the unit to move alone. " If I jump out, ten jumps in." With most of the men, that remark concludes the subject. And yet, especially among the women, there is a slow disturbance—something that is not yet rebellion, and not yet hope, that seems to hold the dim promise of both. The waters are troubled, though one hears some very contradictory accounts of the appearance of the angel.

INDEX.

THE END.

European Sociology

An Arno Press Collection

Barth, Hans. **Wahrheit Und Ideologie.** 1945

Bayet, Albert. **Le Suicide Et La Morale.** 1922

Borkenau, Franz. **Der Übergang Vom Feudalen Zum Bürgerlichen Weltbild.** 1934

Bouglé, C[elestin]. **Bilan De La Sociologie Française Contemporaine.** 1935

Briefs, Goetz A. **The Proletariat.** 1937

Croner, Fritz. **Soziologie Der Angestellten.** 1962

Czarnowski, S[tefan]. **Le Culte Des Héros Et Ses Conditions Sociales:** Saint Patrick; Héros National De L'Irlande, 1919

Davy, Georges. **La Foi Jurée.** 1922

Ehrlich, Eugen. **Fundamental Principles Of The Sociology Of Law.** 1936

Fourastié, Jean. **The Causes Of Wealth.** 1960

Geiger, Theodor. **Aufgaben Und Stellung Der Intelligenz In Der Gesellschaft.** 1949

Geiger, Theodor. **Die Klassengesellschaft Im Schmelztiegel.** 1949

Geiger, Theodor. **Demokratie Ohne Dogma.** [1963]

Granet, Marcel. **La Pensée Chinoise.** 1934

Graunt, John. **Natural And Political Observations Mentioned In A Following Index, And Made Upon The Bills of Mortality.** 1662

Gumplowicz, Ludwig. **The Outlines of Sociology.** 1899

Guyau, M[arie Jean]. **L'Art Au Point De Vue Sociologique.** 1920

Halbwachs, Maurice. **Les Causes Du Suicide.** 1930

Halbwachs, Maurice. **Les Cadres Sociaux De La Mémoire.** 1952

Hobhouse, L[eonard] T., G[erald] C. Wheeler and M[orris]
Ginsberg. **The Material Culture And Social Institutions
Of The Simpler Peoples.** 1915

Hubert, René. **Les Sciences Sociales Dans L'Encyclopédie.** 1923

Jeudwine, J[ohn] W. **The Foundations Of Society And The Land.**
1925

Katz, John. **The Will To Civilization.** 1938

Lazarsfeld, Paul F. et al. **Jugend Und Beruf.** 1931

Le Bras, Gabriel. **Études De Sociologie Religieuse.** 1955/56
Two volumes in one.

Lecky, William Edward Hartpole. **History Of European Morals
From Augustus To Charlemagne.** 1921. Two volumes in one.

Lederer, Emil. **Die Privatangestellten In Der Modernen
Wirtschaftsentwicklung.** 1912

Le Play, F[rédérick]. **Le Réforme Sociale En France Déduite
De L'Observation Comparée Des Peuples Européens.** 1864.
Two volumes in one.

Levenstein, Adolf. **Die Arbeiterfrage.** 1912

Maine, Henry Sumner. **Dissertations On Early Law And Custom.**
1886

Martin Saint-Léon, Etienne. **Histoire Des Corporations De
Metiers.** 1922

Michels, Roberto. **Il Proletariato E La Borghesia Nel Movimento
Socialista Italiano.** 1908

Morselli, Henry. **Suicide.** 1882

Mosca, Gaetano. **Partiti E Sindacati Nella Crisi Del Regime
Parlamentare.** 1949

Niceforo, Alfredo. **Kultur Und Fortschritt Im Spiegel Der Zahlen.**
1930

Palyi, Melchior, ed. **Hauptprobleme Der Soziologie.** 1923.
Two volumes in one.

Picavet, F[rançois Joseph]. **Les Idéologues.** 1891

Ratzenhofer, Gustav. **Die Sociologische Erkenntnis.** 1898

Renner, Karl. **Wandlungen Der Modernen Gesellschaft.** 1953

Rigaudias-Weiss, Hilde. **Les Enquêtes Ouvrières En France Entre 1830 Et 1848.** 1936

Robson, William A. **Civilisation And The Growth Of Law.** 1935

Rowntree, B. Seebohm and May Kendall. **How The Labourer Lives.** 1913

Savigny, Frederick Charles von. **Of The Vocation Of Our Age For Legislation And Jurisprudence.** 1831

Scheler, Max, ed. **Versuche Zu Einer Soziologie Des Wissens.** 1924

Segerstedt, Torgny T. **Die Macht Des Wortes.** 1947

Siegfried, André. **Tableau Politique De La France De L'Ouest Sous La Troisieme Republique.** 1913

Sighele, Scipio. **Psychologie Des Sectes.** 1898

Sombart, Werner. **Krieg Und Kapitalismus.** 1913

Sorel, Georges. **Matériaux D'Une Théorie Du Prolétariat.** 1921

Steinmetz, S[ebald] Rudolf. **Soziologie Des Krieges.** 1929

Tingsten, Herbert. **Political Behavior.** 1937

Vierkandt, Alfred. **Gesellschaftslehre.** 1928

Vinogradoff, Paul. **Common-Sense In Law.** [1914]

von Schelting, Alexander. **Max Webers Wissenschaftslehre.** 1934